PANCAKES }

adrianna adarme

the founder of A Cozy Kitchen blog

PANCAKES

72 sweet and savory recipes for the perfect stack

Photographs by Teri Lyn Fisher

st. martin's griffin
new york

www.stmartins.com

Design by Susan Walsh
Production Manager: Adriana Coada

ISBN 978-1-250-01249-4 (trade paperback)
ISBN 978-1-4668-3560-3 (e-book)

First Edition: May 2013

10 9 8 7 6 5 4 3 2 1

To my parents,

Tatiana and German

{ contents

DINNER PANCAKES

{ acknowledgments

It takes a village to write a cookbook! So many people have shown me kindness and helped along the way. Surely, I must name them:

To my mom and dad, and brother, Daniel. Thank you for listenening to my recipe rants, being critical taste testers, part-time dishwashers, and for being supportive and all-around incredible people. You guys are my favorite humans on the planet.

To my editor, BJ, please accept my gratitude for your feedback, knowledge, guidance, and work on this book. And to Jasmine, thank you for your work on this project.

To my literary agent, Danielle, this would still be an idea if it were not for you. Thank you!

Big high-five to design duo Michelle McMillian and Sue Walsh. Thank you for your work in making these pages not only easy to read but so very attractive.

Gigantic hug to photographer Teri Lyn Fisher and food stylist Jenny Park, you two make food look almost too pretty to eat. Almost.

To my dear friends Teri Lyn Fisher, Justin Hantz, Maggie West, Travis Coles, John Gillilan, Chris Stewart, and Cassie Tregellas—y'all are supercool. And to Joshua Pressman, I'm so grateful I found you.

Lastly, I'd like to thank the readers of my blog. Thank you so much for tuning in each week. Your comments, suggestions, and feedback are awesome. I appreciate you all so greatly. Thank you, thank you!

PANCAKES }

introduction

It all started with pancakes. Growing up, Saturday mornings always commenced with me scooting one of our country-style dining table chairs up against the kitchen counter, propping myself up onto it, and mixing together pancake batter at my dad's strict direction. I'd watch him man the griddle, flipping pancakes, one after another. We'd all shuffle to the table—still in our PJ's—and take our seats, dog included. My dad would pile stacks of warm pancakes onto each of our plates and we'd top them off with a heavy hand of maple syrup. It was on those mornings that we felt most like a family. My dad would be reading the sports and business sections of the newspaper; my mom would be scolding me for feeding the dog from the table, while simultaneously telling my brother to stop with the syrup already.

That must sound like an annoyingly idyllic Saturday morning breakfast, but let me assure you that the food had its flaws, starting with the bland store-bought pancake mix. Worse? The syrup, which was loaded with artificial flavors and sugars.

A few years later, on the coattails of the healthy-food movement, my dad changed his tune. Real maple syrup found its place atop a variety of homemade pancakes. Mind you, not all of them were winners; his buckwheat phase was terrifying. Sure, the nutty flavor and texture were OK, but the lead weight made them better suited as a doorstop. Needless to say, my brother and I missed the instant pancake mix. My dad took notice and soon started on a quest in the pursuit of the perfect pancake. I watched, learned, and cooked alongside him as he mastered a myriad of pancake recipes.

When I went off to college in the Deep South, I traded pancakes for different breakfast fare, like grits and thick-cut, salty bacon. It wasn't until

I moved across the country to California into my teeny-tiny Los Angeles apartment that I yearned for those breakfasts that tasted like home. And so, my own pancake quest began.

I simultaneously started my blog, *A Cozy Kitchen* (http://cozykitchen .com), where my pancake obsession is well documented. I quickly learned that people all around the world shared not only my love for breakfast, but specifically pancakes.

I was surprised, at first, though research shows I shouldn't have been, that pancakes were one of the first foods that we as a human species learned how to cook. There's historical evidence that points to prehistoric societies mixing seed flour with milk and eggs, cooking the batter on hot stones, using the heat from the sun, and ending up with something that was round, flat, and edible—a pancake!

Virtually every continent has its version of a pancake—many of which you'll find within the pages of this book: Europe has crêpes and latkes, South America has disk-shaped arepas and cheesey llapingachos, Asia has Korean kimchi pancakes, and Japan has okonomiyaka. The list goes on and on. . . .

Pancakes, despite their form or country of origin, always signify simple, comfort food. Whether it's a puffed German pancake or an applesauce-kissed latke, pancakes have the ability to act as a time machine, taking people backward to their own childhood kitchens and dining room tables, to a space and time that feels warm and rich.

Every recipe in this book follows that same mantra—simple, comforting, and delicious. Most of the recipes can be whipped up in a matter of minutes, using a single bowl, a measuring cup, and a skillet. And since I'm a believer that pancakes should and can be eaten at all times of the day, this book is broken into two main sections—breakfast and dinner. There's a little bit of everything in this book: oftentimes the recipes are indulgent, but they're always fun and sometimes they're even healthy.

My hope is that this book will inspire you to get in the kitchen and make your own pancake memories around crowded tables, sharing and laughing while eating the food you created.

PANCAKE TIPS AND TECHNIQUES

This book is filled with a variety of pancakes—fritters, patties, Dutch babies, crêpes, and of course, American breakfast pancakes. They're all virtually fuss-free and easy to prepare, but achieving a perfect pancake does require a bit of technique. But don't fret! None of the information or directions that follow are difficult or cumbersome. I do, however, believe that proper pancake technique is important, and can make the difference between a heavy, dense pancake and a light, fluffy stack of pancake perfection. Follow these tips and techniques, and you'll be well on your way.

buttermilk: the lowdown

Buttermilk is dreamy in baked goods, quick breads, and pancakes—it imparts a subtle tang while creating a tender, soft crumb. Traditional buttermilk, which isn't easy to find, is the liquid left behind after churning cream into butter. Nowadays, commercial buttermilk, which you can find in most supermarkets, is actually pasteurized, homogenized low-fat milk that has a culture of lactic acid added to it.

buttermilk in a pinch

There are so many mornings when I wake up wanting a stack of pancakes, but find myself buttermilk-less. These moments of pancake desperation have yielded a dependable solution—make my own buttermilk!

powdered buttermilk

When I first came across this powdered stuff, I'll admit I was a bit skeptical. But after further research, I found it contained no crazy chemicals or funny stuff. It was simply dehydrated, traditional buttermilk.

It lasts far longer than liquid buttermilk and to rehydrate it all you'll need is a measuring cup and water. It's quickly become a staple in my pantry, and its uses go much further than just pancakes; I now use it in a variety of sweet treats. Bob's Red Mill carries my favorite Sweet Cream Buttermilk Powder, but you can buy other brands in the supermarket.

vinegar or lemon juice and milk

If you have white vinegar or lemons and milk on hand, this is also another great substitute in a pinch. All you do is add one tablespoon of vinegar or lemon juice to a measuring cup. Top if off with enough milk until the liquid reaches the 1-cup line. Let the milk mixture stand for 5 minutes and then proceed to use it just like the real stuff.

hey, don't overmix that batter!

A common sentence you'll find in many of the recipes in this book is "mix until just combined." What does this really mean, you ask? Simple. If you overmix the batter, you actually overdevelop the gluten in the wheat flour, resulting in tough, rubbery pancakes. Here's how to perfectly mix pancake batter:

To combine the ingredients, you can use a whisk, if you like, but I find that batter gets stuck in the middle of the whisk, so I actually favor using a fork for the whole recipe. Start by adding all of the dry ingredients to a bowl and combine them thoroughly. You'll notice that a lot of recipes in this book call for "melted butter, cooled." It's important that when you combine your wet ingredients they are close in temperature. If your melted butter is hot and you add it to cold milk, the butter will seize and solidify into chunks. A simple solution to this problem is to let the butter cool to room temperature.

In a measuring cup, measure out whatever milk you're using. To the milk, add the egg, room-temperature melted butter, and any other wet ingredients the recipe calls for. Using a fork or whisk, whisk the ingredients together until they're completely combined. Add the combined wet ingredients to the combined dry ingredients; using the same fork, mix them together until you no longer see any specks of flour, and small to medium lumps are visible.

batter too thin or too thick?

Pancake batter is best used right away. If you happen to leave it for an hour or even overnight, you'll notice that it will have thickened. To thin batter, fold in 1 tablespoon of milk at a time, being careful to not overmix. If you need to thicken pancake batter, sift 1 tablespoon of flour at a time over the batter, gently folding it in until it has reached the perfect consistency.

fruit and other mix-ins

My favorite pancakes are simple buttermilk pancakes with fresh wild blueberries. Whether it's bananas, sliced apples, or raspberries, fruit is delicious in pancakes. I've found that the easiest way to add fruit to pancakes is to add the fruit directly onto the pancake after you pour the batter into the skillet. This gives you control of the very important ratio of fruit to pancake. I also found that when I added fruit to the bowl of batter a lot of the fruit would sink to the bottom and/or tint the batter a funky color. Other mix-ins like oats, wheat germ, or nuts are perfectly fine to add to the bowl of batter, just gently mix them in.

size matters

For standard-size pancakes, I like to use a ¼-cup measure. This yields pancakes that are uniform in size, which makes for easy stacking. For silver dollar pancakes, I scoop 1 tablespoon of batter onto the skillet.

temperature is everything

Preheating your griddle, cast-iron skillet, or nonstick skillet is superimportant. If you add batter to a cold skillet, you'll end up with a flat, not-so-cute pancake. Start by preheating the skillet or griddle over medium heat. You can test the heat of the skillet by dropping a few water droplets onto it. When the droplets bead up and dance on the surface, it is ready. Once the skillet is the right temperature, lower the heat to medium, brush the skillet with butter or oil, and add the batter. Often times, after I flip the pancake, I find that I need to readjust the heat to medium-low. Be sure to keep an eye on the temperature, adjusting as you go—not too hot and not too cold.

the oven is your friend

Pancakes are at their most awesome when they go immediately from skillet to plate. This is usually not a problem when you're making pancakes for yourself and another person, but if you find yourself making pancakes for a large group, you'll need a way to keep the cooked pancakes warm. This is when your oven will come in handy! Line a baking sheet with paper towels or a clean kitchen towel and place in a preheated oven set at 200°F. As the pancakes finish cooking in the skillet, transfer them to the oven, placing them in one layer on the baking sheet. They'll stay warm in the oven and hold their perkiness for up to 10 or 15 minutes.

lots of maple syrup on top, please!

Warm, rich maple syrup is glorious atop a stack of pancakes. But what do the grades mean? And is there really a difference between pure maple syrup and flavored maple syrup?

Here's the lowdown: Maple syrup comes from the sap of black, sugar, or red maple trees. The tree is pierced, allowing the sap to run out; then it's contained and goes through a boiling process, which develops the concentration of flavors. This is when the "grading system" occurs.

Maple syrups comes in five grades: AA, A, B, C, and D. Grades AA and A are most common with pancakes. You'll find that the rest of the grades are richer, darker, and more expensive, making them more ideal for cooking. Grade AA, also known as "fancy," is the lightest and most subtle in flavor. Grade A is broken into three more categories: Light Amber, Medium Amber, and Dark Amber.

So, which one is better? There's no right answer. It's simply a matter of personal preference. Try a few and decide for yourself. But stay away from syrups promising "maple flavor"; they're usually bottles of high fructose corn syrup spiked with a chemical that mocks the flavor of real maple syrup.

a note about salt

Except for the recipes that specify kosher salt, my preference is to use a fine-grain salt (like from Hain Pure Foods). The flavor tends to be a bit more agreeable and cleaner, but table salt works just as fine, too.

PANCAKE TOOLS AND SUPPLIES

what should I cook my pancakes on?

If you're lucky enough to have a stove with a built-in griddle, by all means use it! A two-burner griddle, electric griddle, cast-iron skillet, or nonstick skillet work great.

cast-iron confessions

Every single recipe in this book (minus the popovers) can be made using a cast-iron skillet. This workhorse of a pan is awesome for everything from searing a steak to baking a cake, and of course it's perfect for pancakes, fritters, Dutch Babies, and frying up latkes. Lodge makes a great one, which comes preseasoned. "Seasoning" is simply another word for oiling and baking a cast-iron skillet. If yours didn't come preseasoned, or if you need to reseason it along the way, here's how:

Start by cleaning your cast-iron skillet with hot water and soap. If

there are bits of food or rust on the surface of the skillet, scrub it using a stiff brush or sponge. Rinse and dry the pan thoroughly.

Preheat your oven to 350°F. Pour a few teaspoons of vegetable oil into the cast-iron skillet and, using a paper towel, spread it around the surface and up the sides of the skillet. Transfer the skillet to the oven facedown on the middle rack. Place a sheet of aluminum foil on the rack beneath to catch any dripping. Bake the cookware for one hour. Turn off the oven and allow the skillet to come to room temperature. When a cast-iron skillet is properly seasoned, you'll notice that the surface of the skillet will be smooth with a subtle sheen. To clean a seasoned cast-iron skillet, avoid using water and soap, and instead simply add a few tablespoons of coarse salt to the skillet and scrub clean with a paper towel.

bowls   Most recipes in this book require only one medium bowl. I favor the stainless-steel variety that you can find at restaurant supply stores. They're inexpensive and really sturdy.

liquid measuring cups   For most breakfast pancakes, I mix all of my wet ingredients in a 2-cup measuring cup. I like eliminating cleanup whenever I can.

pancake spatula   I've tried a variety of fancy spatulas that promised all sorts of crazy things. None of them came through on their promise. I found that all you really need in a pancake spatula is for it to be about 4-inches wide, thin, and made of silicone, so it doesn't melt.

fish spatula   A fish spatula is a thin, flexible, stainless-steel spatula that's about 3 inches wide and 6 inches long. It's perfect for panfrying since the slots allow the oil to fall back into the pan. I used it for almost every recipe in the dinner section of this book.

muffin pan   All of the popover recipes you'll find in this book will work perfectly with a popover pan, but guess what? You don't need one. Your basic 12-cup muffin pan works just as well.

BASIC PANCAKE RECIPES

These four pancake recipes are what I like to consider classics. They're all perfect on their own, but I encourage you to use them like a canvas, customizing them as you see fit. Add chocolate chips, berries, nuts, or other fruit—make them your very own.

buttermilk pancakes }

Makes 8 pancakes

1. In a medium bowl, mix together the flour, sugar, baking powder, baking soda, and salt.

2. In a measuring cup or small bowl, measure out the buttermilk. Add the egg, melted butter, and vanilla and beat until thoroughly combined.

3. All at once, add the wet ingredients to the dry ingredients and mix until just combined. The batter should have some small to medium lumps.

4. Preheat your skillet over medium heat and brush with 1½ teaspoons of butter or a teaspoon of vegetable oil. Using a ¼-cup measure, scoop the batter onto the warm skillet. Cook for 2 to 3 minutes until small bubbles form on the surface of the pancakes, and then flip. Reduce the heat to medium-low and cook on the opposite sides for 1 to 2 minutes, or until golden brown.

5. Transfer the cooked pancakes to a baking sheet and place in a preheated 200°F oven to keep warm. Repeat the process with the remaining batter, adding more butter or vegetable oil to the skillet when needed. Serve immediately.

DRY MIX

1 cup all-purpose flour

2 tablespoons sugar

1 teaspoon baking powder

1 teaspoon baking soda

¼ teaspoon salt

WET MIX

1 cup plus 2 tablespoons buttermilk, shaken

1 large egg

2 tablespoons unsalted butter, melted and cooled

1 teaspoon pure vanilla extract

Butter or vegetable oil, for the skillet

vegan pancakes

DRY MIX
1 cup all-purpose flour

1 tablespoon baking powder

¼ teaspoon salt

WET MIX
1 cup almond or soy milk

1 tablespoon agave nectar

1 teaspoon pure vanilla extract

Vegetable oil, for the skillet

Makes 6 pancakes

1. In a medium bowl, mix together the flour, baking powder, and salt.

2. In a measuring cup or small bowl, measure out the milk. Add the agave and vanilla and beat until thoroughly combined.

3. All at once, add the wet ingredients to the dry ingredients and mix until just combined. The batter should have some small to medium lumps.

4. Preheat your skillet over medium heat and brush with 1 teaspoon of vegetable oil. Using a ¼-cup measure, scoop the batter onto the warm skillet. Cook for 3 to 4 minutes until small bubbles form on the surface of the pancakes, and then flip. Reduce the heat to medium-low and cook on the opposite sides for 1 to 2 minutes, or until golden brown.

5. Transfer the cooked pancakes to a baking sheet and place in a preheated 200°F oven to keep warm. Repeat the process with the remaining batter, adding more vegetable oil to the skillet when needed. Serve immediately.

gluten-free pancakes

DRY MIX

¾ cup rice flour

2 tablespoons almond flour

¼ cup tapioca starch

2 tablespoons sugar

1 teaspoon baking powder

½ teaspoon baking soda

¼ teaspoon salt

WET MIX

1 cup buttermilk, shaken

1 large egg

1 tablespoon unsalted butter, melted and cooled

1 teaspoon pure vanilla extract

Butter or vegetable oil, for the skillet

1. In a medium bowl, sift together the flours, tapioca starch, sugar, baking powder, baking soda, and salt.

2. In a measuring cup or small bowl, measure out the buttermilk. Add the egg, butter, and vanilla and beat until thoroughly combined.

3. All at once, add the wet ingredients to the dry ingredients and mix until just combined. The batter should have some small to medium lumps.

4. Preheat your skillet over medium heat and brush with 1½ teaspoons of butter or ½ teaspoon of vegetable oil. Using a ¼-cup measure, scoop the batter onto the warm skillet. Cook for 3 to 4 minutes until small bubbles form on the surface of the pancakes, and then flip. Reduce the heat to medium-low and cook on the opposite sides for 1 to 2 minutes, or until golden brown.

5. Transfer the cooked pancakes to a baking sheet and place in a preheated 200°F oven to keep warm. Repeat the process with the remaining batter, adding more butter or vegetable oil to the skillet when needed. Serve immediately.

crêpes

2 large eggs, at room temperature

1 cup whole milk, at room temperature

¼ cup water

2 tablespoons unsalted butter, melted and cooled

1 cup all-purpose flour

2 tablespoons sugar

⅛ teaspoon salt

Butter, for the crêpe pan

1. To the jar of a blender, add the eggs, milk, water, and melted butter and pulse for a few seconds until the liquids are combined. Add the flour, sugar, and salt and pulse for about 10 seconds, or until the flour is incorporated, being sure not to overblend. Transfer the batter to a bowl and cover with plastic wrap. Place the batter in the refrigerator for an hour to rest.

2. Place a crêpe pan, or a nonstick skillet, over medium heat. Brush the pan with a very light coating of butter. Add 2 ounces (¼ cup) of batter to the center of the pan, and swirl it around until the bottom is coated evenly. Cook until the edges of the crêpe pull away from the pan, 1 to 2 minutes. Flip and cook on the opposite side for another 30 seconds. Transfer the crêpe to a baking sheet and place in a preheated 200°F oven to keep warm. Repeat the process with the remaining batter, adding more butter to the skillet when needed. Serve immediately.

BREAKFAST
PANCAKES

If I had my way, I'd eat breakfast for breakfast, lunch, and dinner. It's a fun meal. It's satisfying and comforting. And breakfast is always, always necessary. This collection of breakfast recipes makes it so there's a pancake for every person, every mood, and every occasion.

orange and chocolate chip pancakes

Makes 8 pancakes

When recipe testing, you always need a recipe taster. This person should be critical, trustworthy, and brutally honest. Enter: my father. He has, on more than one occasion, told me that I have fed him the worst—the WORST!!—food he's ever consumed. On the flip side, when he loves something, his praises, in my book, are worth gold. He'll badger me for details, inquire about complementing flavors and go on and on about the dish for hours. He tried every pancake in this book and these Orange and Chocolate Chip Pancakes are his all-time favorite.

1. In a medium bowl, mix together the flour, sugar, baking powder, baking soda, orange zest, and salt.
2. In a measuring cup or small bowl, measure out the buttermilk. Add the egg and melted butter and beat until thoroughly combined.
3. All at once, add the wet ingredients to the dry ingredients and mix until just combined. The batter should have some small to medium lumps.
4. Preheat your skillet over medium heat and brush with 1½ teaspoons of butter or a teaspoon of oil. Using a ¼-cup measure, scoop the batter onto the warm skillet. Add 10 to 12 chocolate chips to each pancake, gently pressing them into the pancake. Cook for 2 to 3 minutes until small bubbles form on the surface, and then flip. Reduce the heat to medium-low and cook on the opposite sides for about 1 minute, or until golden brown.
5. Transfer the cooked pancakes to a baking sheet and place in a preheated 200°F oven to keep warm. Repeat the process with the remaining batter, adding more butter or vegetable oil to the skillet when needed. Serve immediately.

DRY MIX

1 cup all-purpose flour

2 tablespoons sugar

1 teaspoon baking powder

1 teaspoon baking soda

1 teaspoon finely grated orange zest

⅛ teaspoon salt

WET MIX

1¼ cups buttermilk, shaken

1 large egg

1 tablespoon unsalted butter, melted and cooled

ADD IN

¼ cup milk chocolate chips

Butter or vegetable oil, for the skillet

honey and oat pancakes

DRY MIX

½ cup all-purpose flour

¼ cup whole-wheat flour

1 tablespoon baking powder

½ teaspoon ground cinnamon

¼ teaspoon salt

WET MIX

1 cup whole milk

3 tablespoons honey

1 large egg

MIX-IN

¼ cup rolled oats

Butter or vegetable oil, for the skillet

Makes 6 pancakes

Sure, I have a food blog, which means I practically cook and write for a living. But I'm not above cereal for dinner; it's actually the polar opposite. A bowl of cereal for dinner is ritualistic for me: the opening of the cabinets, the ice cold milk, the eating whilst cuddling on the couch watching bad television—it's a dreamy way for me to spend an evening. You should try it! These pancakes were inspired by one of my favorite cereals, Honey Bunches of Oats. The honey flavor is pronounced and the rolled oats give it an awesome crunch.

1. In a medium bowl, mix together the flours, baking powder, cinnamon, and salt.
2. In a measuring cup or small bowl, measure out the milk. Add the honey and egg and beat for 1 minute, or until the honey has completely dissolved into the milk.
3. All at once, add the wet ingredients to the dry ingredients and mix until just combined. The batter should have some small to medium lumps. Gently fold in the rolled oats.
4. Preheat your skillet over medium heat and brush with 1½ teaspoons of butter or a teaspoon of vegetable oil. Using a ¼-cup measure, scoop the batter onto the warm skillet. Cook for 2 to 3 minutes until small bubbles form on the surface of the pancakes, and then flip. Reduce the heat to medium-low and cook on the opposite sides for about 1 minute, or until golden brown.
5. Transfer the cooked pancakes to a baking sheet and place in a preheated 200°F oven to keep warm. Repeat the process with the remaining batter, adding more butter or vegetable oil to the skillet when needed. Serve immediately.

whole-wheat pancakes

Makes 8 pancakes

DRY MIX

½ cup all-purpose flour

½ cup whole-wheat flour

1 tablespoon baking powder

⅛ teaspoon salt

WET MIX

¾ cup whole milk

1½ tablespoons agave nectar

1 large egg

MIX-IN

¼ cup wheat germ

Butter or vegetable oil, for the skillet

HEADS-UP

Wheat germ is full of vitamins like Vitamin E, zinc, and magnesium, and is a good source of fiber.

In the early '90s, my parents jumped on the health bandwagon; our refrigerator got, what I like to call a "hippie makeover." Whole milk was swapped out for soy and rice milk, dessert went from cookies to fresh berries, and whole wheat and buckwheat replaced our traditional Saturday morning buttermilk pancakes. Obviously, my brother Daniel and I were not excited about this. My dad's whole-wheat pancakes were heavy, mealy, and all-around gross, basically the antithesis of what a pancake should be. The trick, as I've discovered, to making delicious whole-wheat pancakes is to include some all-purpose flour. This stack is the perfect combination of healthy and nutty, while still light and fluffy.

1. In a medium bowl, mix together the flours, baking powder, and salt.
2. In a measuring cup or small bowl, measure out the milk. Add the agave and egg and beat until completely incorporated into the milk.
3. All at once, add the wet ingredients to the dry ingredients and mix until just combined. The batter should have some small to medium lumps. Gently fold in the wheat germ.
4. Preheat your skillet over medium heat and brush with 1½ teaspoons of butter or a teaspoon of vegetable oil. Using a ¼-cup measure, scoop the batter onto the warm skillet. Cook for 2 to 3 minutes until small bubbles form on the surface of the pancakes, and then flip. Reduce the heat to medium-low and cook on the opposite sides for about 1 minute, or until golden brown.
5. Transfer the cooked pancakes to a baking sheet and place in a preheated 200°F oven to keep warm. Repeat the process with the remaining batter, adding more butter or vegetable oil to the skillet when needed. Serve immediately.

red velvet silver dollars

DRY MIX

1 cup all-purpose flour

3 tablespoons sugar

2 tablespoons unsweetened Dutch-process cocoa powder

1 teaspoon baking powder

1 teaspoon baking soda

¼ teaspoon salt

WET MIX

1 ¼ cups buttermilk, shaken

1 large egg

1 tablespoon unsalted butter, melted and cooled

1 tablespoon red food coloring

1 teaspoon pure vanilla extract

Butter or vegetable oil, for the skillet

There's nothing special about red velvet cupcakes. They're about as ubiquitous as the cupcake itself. Yet their overexposure doesn't make me love them any less. When done to perfection, a red velvet cupcake is moist, chocolatey, and topped with the fluffiest tangy cream cheese icing. This pancake version is all of those things . . . except we're calling it breakfast.

1. In a medium bowl, mix together the flour, sugar, cocoa powder, baking powder, baking soda, and salt.
2. In a measuring cup or small bowl, measure out the buttermilk. Add the egg, melted butter, red food coloring, and vanilla and beat until thoroughly combined.
3. All at once, add the wet ingredients to the dry ingredients and mix until just combined. The batter should have some small to medium lumps.
4. Preheat your skillet over medium heat and brush with 1½ teaspoons of butter or a teaspoon of vegetable oil. Using a tablespoon measure, scoop the batter onto the warm skillet. Cook for 2 to 3 minutes until small bubbles form on the surface of the pancakes, and then flip. Reduce the heat to medium-low and cook on the opposite sides for about 1 minute, or until golden brown.
5. Transfer the cooked pancakes to a baking sheet and place in a preheated 200°F oven to keep warm. Repeat the process with the remaining batter, adding more butter or vegetable oil to the skillet when needed. Serve immediately.

apple pie pancakes

Makes 8 pancakes

Every year, when fall—and also my birthday—rolls around I convince my friends to pile in a car with me and drive an hour east of Los Angeles to Riley Apple Farm. There's initially a lot of whining, since going requires an early wake-up time, but once everyone is outdoors, picking and eating their very own apples, they change their tune. I first made these pancakes a few years ago when I had returned from the apple-picking day trip and had many more apples than I knew what to do with. These pancakes have all the spices and warmth you'd find in an apple pie, minus the fussy pie dough and baking time.

1. In a medium bowl, mix together the flour, sugar, baking powder, cinnamon, salt, and nutmeg.
2. In a measuring cup or small bowl, measure out the milk. Add the egg, melted butter, and vanilla and beat until combined.
3. All at once, add the wet ingredients to the dry ingredients and mix until just combined. The batter should have some small to medium lumps. Gently fold in the grated apple.
4. Preheat your skillet over medium heat and brush with 1½ teaspoons of butter or a teaspoon of vegetable oil. Using a ¼-cup measure, scoop the batter onto the warm skillet. Cook for 1 to 2 minutes until small bubbles form on the surface of the pancakes, and then flip. Reduce the heat to medium-low and cook on the opposite sides for about 1 minute, or until golden brown.
5. Transfer the cooked pancakes to a baking sheet and place in a preheated 200°F oven to keep warm. Repeat the process with the remaining batter, adding more butter or vegetable oil to the skillet when needed. Serve immediately.

DRY MIX

1 cup all-purpose flour

2 tablespoons light brown sugar

1 teaspoon baking powder

1 teaspoon ground cinnamon

⅛ teaspoon salt

⅛ teaspoon freshly grated nutmeg

WET MIX

1 cup whole milk

1 large egg

1 tablespoon unsalted butter, melted and cooled

1 teaspoon pure vanilla extract

MIX-IN

1 cup peeled and grated apple (about 1 medium apple)

Butter or vegetable oil, for the skillet

cranberry–brown butter pancakes

BROWN BUTTER

3 tablespoons unsalted butter, cubed

DRY MIX

1 cup all-purpose flour

2 tablespoons sugar

1 teaspoon baking powder

1 teaspoon baking soda

½ teaspoon salt

WET MIX

1¼ cups buttermilk, shaken

1 large egg

½ teaspoon pure vanilla extract

ADD IN

1 cup fresh cranberries

Butter or vegetable oil, for the skillet

Browning butter, while as easy as can be, requires a watchful eye, since there's a fine line between brown, nutty, delicious butter, and straight-up burnt. These pancakes' rich flavor works wonders with the tart cranberries. As the seasons change, I love to swap them out with everything from winter citrus to fresh summer cherries.

1. Place the butter in a small saucepan over medium-low heat. When the butter melts, swirl the pan occasionally. You'll notice that as the butter melts, the white foam will subside. This is the water cooking itself out of the butter. Keep a watchful eye on it and when brown specks begin to appear throughout the butter, remove it from the heat, set aside, and allow it to come to room temperature.

2. In a medium bowl, mix together the flour, sugar, baking powder, baking soda, and salt.

3. In a measuring cup or small bowl, measure out the buttermilk. Add the egg, vanilla, and brown butter and beat until thoroughly combined.

4. All at once, add the wet ingredients to the dry ingredients and mix until just combined. The batter should have some small to medium lumps.

5. Preheat your skillet over medium heat and brush with 1½ teaspoons of butter or a teaspoon of vegetable oil. Using a ¼-cup measure, scoop the batter onto the warm skillet. Add 6 to 8 cranberries to each pancake, gently pressing them into the pancake. Cook for 2 to 3 minutes until small bubbles form on the surface of the pancakes, and then flip. Reduce the heat to medium-low and cook on the opposite sides for about 1 minute, or until golden brown.

6. Transfer the cooked pancakes to a baking sheet and place in a preheated 200°F oven to keep warm. Repeat the process with the remaining batter, adding more butter or vegetable oil to the skillet when needed. Serve immediately.

chocolate hazelnut pancakes

HAZELNUTS

¼ cup whole
hazelnuts

DRY MIX

1 cup all-purpose flour

2 tablespoons sugar

1 tablespoon baking
powder

⅛ teaspoon salt

WET MIX

1 cup whole milk

1 large egg

1 tablespoon unsalted
butter, melted and
cooled

¼ cup Nutella

Butter or vegetable oil,
for the skillet

When berry season rolls around, all I want do is sit on the couch, watch trashy television, and smother everything from strawberries to blackberries with Nutella—it's a total waste of a beautiful, summer afternoon, I know. My love for this Italian hazelnut spread inspired these pancakes. These pancakes are chocolatey and rich, while the toasted and chopped hazelnuts give this fluffy stack an awesome crunch.

1. Preheat the oven to 350°F. Spread out hazelnuts in one layer on a baking sheet and toast for 10 to 15 minutes, or until the nuts are lightly colored and skins are blistered. Pour the nuts onto a clean kitchen towel. Gather the towel around the nuts and rub gently to loosen the skins, continuing until they fall off. Transfer the peeled hazelnuts to a food processor and pulse for 30 seconds until coarsely ground. Set aside.

2. In a medium bowl, mix together the flour, sugar, baking powder, and salt.

3. In a measuring cup or small bowl, measure out the milk. Add the egg, melted butter, and Nutella and beat for 1 to 2 minutes until the Nutella is thoroughly incorporated.

4. All at once, add the wet ingredients to the dry ingredients and mix until just combined. The batter should have some small to medium lumps. Gently fold in ¼ cup of ground hazelnuts. Reserve the rest for the topping.

5. Preheat your skillet over medium heat and brush with 1½ teaspoons of butter or a teaspoon of vegetable oil. Using a ¼-cup measure, scoop the batter onto the warm skillet. Cook for 2 to 3 minutes until small bubbles form on the surface of the pancakes, and then flip.

Reduce the heat to medium-low and cook on the opposite sides for about 1 minute, or until golden brown.

6. Transfer the cooked pancakes to a baking sheet and place in a preheated 200°F oven to keep warm. Repeat the process with the remaining batter, adding more butter or vegetable oil to the skillet when needed. Serve immediately.

carrot cake pancakes

DRY MIX

DRY MIX

1 cup all-purpose flour

2 tablespoons light brown sugar

1½ teaspoons ground cinnamon

1 teaspoon baking powder

1 teaspoon baking soda

½ teaspoon salt

⅛ teaspoon freshly grated nutmeg

WET MIX

1¼ cups buttermilk, shaken

1 large egg

1 teaspoon pure vanilla extract

MIX-INS

¾ cup peeled and grated carrots

¼ cup diced pineapple

⅛ cup chopped pecans

Butter or vegetable oil, for the skillet

Makes 8 pancakes

Going to college in the South turned me into an ardent carrot cake eater and critic. This recipe is inspired by the best carrot cake I've ever had. It was from a random diner, whose name I can't even recall, but it was everything carrot cake should be: moist, studded with nuts, pineapple, fresh grated carrots, and topped with a fluffy cream cheese icing. This pancake version bundles everything that was perfect with that cake and makes it acceptable to eat for breakfast.

1. In a medium bowl, mix together the flour, sugar, cinnamon, baking powder, baking soda, salt, and nutmeg.
2. In a measuring cup or small bowl, measure out the buttermilk. Add the egg and vanilla and beat until thoroughly combined.
3. All at once, add the wet ingredients to the dry ingredients and mix until just combined. The batter should have some small to medium lumps. Gently fold in the grated carrots, pecans, and pineapple.
4. Preheat your skillet over medium heat and brush with 1½ teaspoons of butter or a teaspoon of vegetable oil. Using a ¼-cup measure, scoop the batter onto the warm skillet. Cook for 2 to 3 minutes until small bubbles form on the surface of the pancakes, and then flip. Reduce the heat to medium-low and cook on the opposite sides for 1 to 2 minutes, or until golden brown.
5. Transfer the cooked pancakes to a baking sheet and place in a preheated 200°F oven to keep warm. Repeat the process with the remaining batter, adding more butter or vegetable oil to the skillet when needed. Serve immediately.

PRO-TIP

I love to top these pancakes with Cream Cheese Glaze (page 148).

vanilla bean dutch baby

Makes one 10-inch Dutch baby

When Dutch babies exit the oven, they're showstoppers. Their golden edges and lopsided, yet pillowy, risen center will make people's jaws drop—and rightfully so! This Dutch baby uses one vanilla bean, two ways: in the batter and added to the sugar that's sprinkled on top.

1. Preheat the oven for 2 to 3 minutes to 400°F. Place a 10-inch cast-iron skillet in the oven to preheat.

2. In a medium bowl, whisk together eggs, milk, and the vanilla bean seeds from ½ of the pod until thoroughly combined. Add the flour, sugar, and salt and whisk until lumps are barely visible. The batter will be thin.

3. Carefully remove the hot skillet from the oven and add the butter, and swirl it around until melted. Pour the batter into the skillet, return it to the oven, and bake the pancake for 30 minutes, or until the center is puffed and the edges are golden brown.

4. Meanwhile, whisk together the sugar and the vanilla bean seeds from the remaining half pod. Lightly brush the top of the cooked Dutch baby with the melted butter and liberally sprinkle the vanilla-sugar mixture on top. Serve immediately.

BATTER

3 large eggs, at room temperature

⅔ cup plus 3 tablespoons whole milk, at room temperature

1 vanilla bean, split lengthwise scraped, ½ reserved for the topping

⅔ cup all-purpose flour

3 tablespoons sugar

⅛ teaspoon salt

4 tablespoons (½ stick) unsalted butter, cubed

TOPPING

¼ tablespoon unsalted butter, melted

2 tablespoons sugar

banana bread pancakes }

Makes 8 pancakes

Bananas are a staple on my shopping list, yet I always end up forgetting about them until they're too unattractive to want to eat. If this happens to you, too, not to worry. This stack of banana and walnut-studded goodness is the perfect solution for those ugly, brown, and forgotten-about bananas that are most likely sitting on your kitchen counter this very second.

1. In a medium bowl, mix together the flour, sugar, baking powder, baking soda, cinnamon, and salt.

2. In a small bowl, combine the mashed banana and vegetable oil. Add the egg, buttermilk, and vanilla and mix until thoroughly combined.

3. All at once, add the wet ingredients to the dry ingredients and mix until just combined. The batter should have some small to medium lumps. Gently fold in the walnuts.

4. Preheat your skillet over medium heat and brush with 1½ teaspoons of butter or a teaspoon of vegetable oil. Using a ¼-cup measure, scoop the batter onto the warm skillet. Cook for 2 to 3 minutes until small bubbles form on the surface of the pancakes, and then flip. Reduce the heat to medium-low and cook on the opposite sides for 1 to 2 minutes, or until golden brown.

5. Transfer the cooked pancakes to a baking sheet and place in a preheated 200°F oven to keep warm. Repeat the process with the remaining batter, adding more butter or vegetable oil to the skillet when needed. Serve immediately.

DRY MIX

1 cup all-purpose flour

1 tablespoon light brown sugar

1 teaspoon baking powder

1 teaspoon baking soda

¼ teaspoon ground cinnamon

¼ teaspoon salt

WET MIX

1 cup mashed ripe bananas (about 2 bananas)

¼ cup vegetable oil

1 cup buttermilk, shaken

1 large egg

1 teaspoon pure vanilla extract

MIX-IN

⅓ cup walnuts, chopped

Butter or vegetable oil, for the skillet

maple bacon pancakes

MAPLE BACON

5 slices thick-cut bacon

3 tablespoons maple syrup

DRY MIX

1 cup all-purpose flour

1 tablespoon sugar

1 teaspoon baking powder

1 teaspoon baking soda

⅛ teaspoon salt

WET MIX

1 cup buttermilk, shaken

¼ cup pure maple syrup

1 large egg

1 tablespoon unsalted butter, melted and cooled

Butter or vegetable oil, for the skillet

Makes 8 pancakes

I'm what you would call a dreamer. I can sit and stare at the wall and dream for hours upon hours. I sometimes dream about the fancy things I want out of life; but mostly I dream about moving far into the country, with a little family I created, onto a farm we could call our own. It's on this farm that I get to fulfill a weird lifelong dream of mine: to have a pet teacup pig. I'd give him an incredibly proper name like Richard or Franklin. And we'd spend our afternoons playing in the mud, hanging out by the fire, and cuddling when it's cold out. If my dream ever comes true, I vow to never eat these pancakes again, because, well, that'd be just rude.

1. Preheat the oven to 400°F. On a parchment paper–lined baking sheet, place the bacon slices side by side and brush both sides with maple syrup. Bake for 15 to 20 minutes until the bacon becomes golden brown and crispy. Remove from the oven and drain on paper towels, being careful with the hot grease. When the bacon cools, chop it into bite-size pieces.

2. In a medium bowl, mix together the flour, sugar, baking powder, baking soda, and kosher salt.

3. In a measuring cup or small bowl, measure out the buttermilk. Add the maple syrup, egg, and melted butter and beat until thoroughly combined.

4. All at once, add the wet ingredients to the dry ingredients and mix until just combined. The batter should have some small to medium lumps. Gently fold in the diced bacon.

5. Preheat your skillet over medium heat and brush with 1½ teaspoons of butter or a teaspoon of vegetable oil. Using a ¼-cup measure, scoop the batter onto the warm skillet. Cook for 2 to 3 minutes until small bubbles form on the surface of the pancakes, and then flip. Reduce the heat to medium-low and cook on the opposite sides for 1 to 2 minutes, or until golden brown.

6. Transfer the cooked pancakes to a baking sheet and place in a preheated 200°F oven to keep warm. Repeat the process with the remaining batter, adding more butter or vegetable oil to the skillet when needed. Serve immediately.

coffee pancakes }

My coffee addiction is borderline scary; actually, there's nothing borderline about it—it's just plain scary. These pancakes are a direct reflection of my long-lasting love affair. There's no fancy coffee shop roast in these pancakes—just instant coffee granules. I couldn't be paid to drink the stuff, though I do find it great to bake with. It gives these pancakes a concentrated coffee flavor without a ground or granule in sight.

1. In a medium bowl, mix together the flour, sugar, baking powder, baking soda, and salt.
2. In a measuring cup or small bowl, measure out the buttermilk. Add the egg, instant coffee granules, and melted butter and beat until thoroughly combined.
3. All at once, add the wet ingredients to the dry ingredients and mix until just combined. The batter should have some small to medium lumps.
4. Preheat your skillet over medium heat and brush with 1½ teaspoons of butter or a teaspoon of vegetable oil. Using a ¼-cup measure, scoop the batter onto the warm skillet. Cook for 2 to 3 minutes until small bubbles form on the surface of the pancakes, and then flip. Reduce the heat to medium-low and cook on the opposite sides for 1 to 2 minutes, or until golden brown.
5. Transfer the cooked pancakes to a baking sheet and place in a preheated 200°F oven to keep warm. Repeat the process with the remaining batter, adding more butter or vegetable oil to the skillet when needed. Serve immediately.

DRY MIX

1 cup all-purpose flour

2 tablespoons sugar

1 teaspoon baking powder

1 teaspoon baking soda

¼ teaspoon salt

WET MIX

1 cup buttermilk, shaken

1 large egg

2 tablespoons instant coffee granules

1 tablespoon unsalted butter, melted and cooled

Butter or vegetable oil, for the skillet

spiced pumpkin pancakes

Makes 8 pancakes

I first made pumpkin pancakes when I was going through a bad breakup. I was on the hunt for some sort of relief in the name of carbs. You can relate, no? Armed with leftover pumpkin puree and a handful of chocolate chips that were living in my cupboards, I whipped up a stack similar to these that didn't really heal my pain—no pancakes are *that* good—but they sure did put a smile on my face.

DRY MIX

¾ cup all-purpose flour

¼ cup whole-wheat flour

2 tablespoons light brown sugar

1 teaspoon baking powder

1 teaspoon baking soda

¼ teaspoon salt

1 teaspoon ground cinnamon

¼ teaspoon freshly grated nutmeg

⅛ teaspoon ground cloves

⅛ teaspoon ground ginger

WET MIX

1 cup buttermilk, shaken

1 large egg

¼ cup canned unsweetened pumpkin puree

½ tablespoon unsalted butter, melted and cooled

Butter or vegetable oil, for the skillet

1. In a medium bowl, mix together the flours, sugar, baking powder, baking soda, salt, cinnamon, nutmeg, cloves, and ginger.

2. In a measuring cup or small bowl, measure out the buttermilk. Add the egg, pumpkin puree, and melted butter and beat until thoroughly combined.

3. All at once, add the wet ingredients to the dry ingredients and mix until just combined. The batter should have some small to medium lumps.

4. Preheat your skillet over medium heat and brush with 1½ teaspoons of butter or a teaspoon of vegetable oil. Using a ¼-cup measure, scoop the batter onto the warm skillet. Cook for 2 to 3 minutes until small bubbles form on the surface of the pancakes, and then flip. Reduce the heat to medium-low and cook on the opposite sides for 1 to 2 minutes, or until golden brown.

5. Transfer the cooked pancakes to a baking sheet and place in a preheated 200°F oven to keep warm. Repeat the process with the remaining batter, adding more butter or vegetable oil to the skillet when needed. Serve immediately.

gingerbread pancakes ⎫

These pancakes taste like Christmas on a plate. When made incorrectly, ginger-bread makes my nose itchy—it's the spices! But these pancakes are the perfect combination of spices and molasses. After eating a plate of these, all you'll want to do is wrap presents in your PJs, while Vince Guaraldi's "A Charlie Brown Christmas" blares in the background.

1. In a medium bowl, mix together the flours, sugar, baking powder, baking soda, cinnamon, ginger, salt, nutmeg, and cloves.

2. In a measuring cup or small bowl, measure out the buttermilk. Add the egg, molasses, and melted butter and beat until combined.

3. All at once, add the wet ingredients to the dry ingredients and mix until just combined. The batter should have some small to medium lumps.

4. Preheat your skillet over medium heat and brush with 1½ teaspoons of butter or a teaspoon of vegetable oil. Using a ¼-cup measure, scoop the batter onto the warm skillet. Cook for 2 to 3 minutes until small bubbles form on the surface of the pancakes, and then flip. Reduce the heat to medium-low and cook on the opposite sides for 2 to 3 minutes, or until golden brown.

5. Transfer the cooked pancakes to a baking sheet and place in a preheated 200°F oven to keep warm. Repeat the process with the remaining batter, adding more butter or vegetable oil to the skillet when needed. Serve immediately.

DRY MIX

¾ cup all-purpose flour

¼ cup whole-wheat flour

3 tablespoons dark brown sugar

1 teaspoon baking powder

1 teaspoon baking soda

1 teaspoon ground cinnamon

½ teaspoon ground ginger

¼ teaspoon salt

⅛ teaspoon freshly grated nutmeg

⅛ teaspoon ground cloves

WET MIX

1 cup buttermilk, shaken

1 large egg

1 tablespoon molasses

½ tablespoon unsalted butter, melted and cooled

Butter or vegetable oil, for the skillet

cinnamon bun pancakes

GLAZE

½ cup confectioners'
sugar, sifted

1 tablespoon whole
milk

¼ teaspoon pure
vanilla extract

DRY MIX

1 cup all-purpose flour

2 tablespoons
granulated sugar

3 teaspoons ground
cinnamon

1 teaspoon baking
powder

1 teaspoon baking
soda

⅛ teaspoon salt

WET MIX

1¼ cup buttermilk,
shaken

1 large egg

1 tablespoon unsalted
butter, melted and
cooled

Butter or vegetable oil,
for the skillet

Makes 8 pancakes

Like most American teenagers, my formative years were spent at the mall with friends (window) shopping at J.Crew, The Gap, and my all-time favorite, Claire's. I was the one in the group that always made sure we ended our retail-rounds at Cinnabon. Their warm cinnamon buns, topped with gooey frosting always made for a successful mall trip. All the girls ate theirs with forks, I used my hands. This pancake version—with no rises and no baking!—is a whole lot easier than baking a batch of cinnamon buns.

1. To make the glaze: Add the confectioners' sugar, milk, and vanilla to a small bowl and whisk vigorously until the mixture is smooth and creamy. If the glaze is either too thin or too thick, simply add more confectioners' sugar or milk to reach a consistency to your liking. Set aside.

2. To make the pancakes: In a medium bowl, mix together the flour, granulated sugar, cinnamon, baking powder, baking soda, and salt.

3. In a measuring cup or small bowl, measure out the buttermilk. Add the egg and melted butter and beat until thoroughly combined.

4. All at once, add the wet ingredients to the dry ingredients and mix until just combined. The batter should have some small to medium lumps.

5. Preheat your skillet over medium heat and brush with 1½ teaspoons of butter or a teaspoon of vegetable oil. Using a ¼-cup measure, scoop the batter onto the warm skillet. Cook for 2 to 3 minutes until small bubbles form on the surface of the pancakes, and then flip.

Reduce the heat to medium-low and cook on the opposite sides for
1 to 2 minutes, or until golden brown.

6. Transfer the cooked pancakes to a baking sheet and place in a
   preheated 200°F oven to keep warm. Repeat the process with the
   remaining batter, adding more butter or vegetable oil to the skillet
   when needed. Serve immediately.

ginger pear pancakes

Makes 8 pancakes

MIX-INS

1 tablespoon unsalted butter

3 tablespoons rolled oats

1 firm pear, peeled, cored, and diced

1 teaspoon freshly squeezed lemon juice

½ teaspoon peeled and grated fresh ginger

DRY MIX

1 cup all-purpose flour

2 tablespoons light brown sugar

1 teaspoon ground cinnamon

1 tablespoon baking powder

¼ teaspoon freshly grated nutmeg

¼ teaspoon salt

WET MIX

1 cup whole milk

1 large egg

Butter or vegetable oil, for the skillet

Baking a crumble shows that you know how to enjoy life. They're casual, fuss-free, and always take advantage of seasonal fruit. These pancakes were inspired by a Ginger Pear Crumble I had at my favorite Los Angeles bakery, Short Cake. This pancake version starts with sautéing rolled oats, sliced pears, and fresh ginger with a pat of butter. This mixture is folded into a spice-laden pancake batter to create the breakfast version of one of my favorite desserts.

1. Melt the butter in a small skillet. Add the pears, rolled oats, lemon juice, and grated ginger and stir to combine. Cook until the pears become tender, 2 to 3 minutes.
2. In a medium bowl, mix together the flour, sugar, cinnamon, baking powder, nutmeg, and salt.
3. In a measuring cup or small bowl, measure out the milk. Add the egg and butter and beat until thoroughly combined.
4. All at once, add the wet ingredients to the dry ingredients and mix until just combined. The batter should have some small to medium lumps. Gently fold in the pear mixture.
5. Preheat your skillet over medium heat and brush with 1½ teaspoons of butter or a teaspoon of vegetable oil. Using a ¼-cup measure, scoop the batter onto the warm skillet. Cook for 2 to 3 minutes until small bubbles form on the surface of the pancakes, and then flip. Reduce the heat to medium-low and cook on the opposite sides for 1 to 2 minutes, or until golden brown.
6. Transfer the cooked pancakes to a baking sheet and place in a preheated 200°F oven to keep warm. Repeat the process with the remaining batter, adding more butter or vegetable oil to the skillet when needed. Serve immediately.

51

buckwheat buttermilk pancakes

Buckwheat gets a bad rap. Poor buckwheat—it really isn't its fault. I'll admit I haven't always been successful cooking with buckwheat, but in this recipe, buckwheat is used in combination with all-purpose flour, which ensures that you'll have a light, fluffy stack while still experiencing its rich, nutty flavor.

1. In a medium bowl, mix together the flours, sugar, baking powder, baking soda, and salt.

2. In a measuring cup or small bowl, measure out the buttermilk. Add the egg and vanilla extract and beat until thoroughly combined.

3. All at once, add the wet ingredients to the dry ingredients and mix until just combined. The batter should have some small to medium lumps.

4. Preheat your skillet over medium heat and brush with 1½ teaspoons of butter or a teaspoon of vegetable oil. Using a ¼-cup measure, scoop the batter onto the warm skillet. Cook for 2 to 3 minutes until small bubbles form on the surface of the pancakes, and then flip. Reduce the heat to medium-low and cook on the opposite sides for 1 to 2 minutes, or until golden brown.

5. Transfer the cooked pancakes to a baking sheet and place in a preheated 200°F oven to keep warm. Repeat the process with the remaining batter, adding more butter or vegetable oil to the skillet when needed. Serve immediately.

DRY MIX

½ cup all-purpose flour

½ cup buckwheat flour

1 tablespoon sugar

1 teaspoon baking powder

1 teaspoon baking soda

¼ teaspoon salt

WET MIX

1¼ cups buttermilk, shaken

1 large egg

½ teaspoon pure vanilla extract

Butter or vegetable oil, for the skillet

chai tea popovers

Makes 12 popovers

Vegetable oil or cooking spray for the muffin pan

BATTER

1½ cups whole milk, at room temperature

3 chai tea bags

1½ tablespoons unsalted butter, melted

1½ cups all-purpose flour

½ teaspoon salt

3 large eggs, at room temperature

HEADS-UP

To bring eggs to room temperature quickly, place them in a bowl with hot water and let stand for 5 minutes.

In college I had a short stint where I gave up coffee and switched to chai tea. I got really into making my own, mixing the perfect amount of spices and steeping them until the tea was just right. These warm popovers remind me of those days. Now I like to enjoy these warm, spiced chai popovers with a strong cup of coffee.

1. Preheat the oven to 350°F. Generously coat a muffin pan with the vegetable oil or spray and set aside.

2. In a small saucepan, bring the milk to a slight simmer. Remove the pan from the heat and add the tea bags. Set aside to infuse for 5 to 7 minutes. Remove the tea bags, transfer the liquid to a measuring cup, and let cool to room temperature.

3. Meanwhile, in a medium bowl, combine the melted butter, flour, salt, and eggs. Add the cooled milk and mix until thoroughly combined. The batter will be thin. Transfer the batter to a measuring cup or a bowl with a spout; this will make it easier to pour the batter into the muffin wells.

4. Preheat the muffin pan in the oven for 2 to 3 minutes. Remove it from the oven and carefully pour the batter into each well, filling them a little more than halfway. Bake for 30 to 35 minutes until tall, puffed, and golden brown.

PRO-TIP

Make sure you add the popovers to a well preheated oven. It's also important that you don't open the oven door to peek! With this recipe, the oven light is your friend.

blueberry ricotta pancakes

Makes 8 pancakes

Gjelina in Venice Beach is one of my favorite spots in Los Angeles to brunch. Every time I go, I tell myself I'm going to get something else, but I always end up with a stack of their blueberry ricotta pancakes. These pancakes are inspired by Gjelina's—they're light, refreshing, and have a wonderful creamy center.

1. In a medium bowl, mix together the flour, sugar, baking powder, and salt.
2. Add the ricotta, milk, egg, lemon zest, vanilla, and butter to a small bowl and mix until smooth.
3. All at once, add the wet ingredients to the dry ingredients and mix until just combined. The batter should have some small to medium lumps.
4. Preheat your skillet over medium heat and brush with 1½ teaspoons of butter or a teaspoon of vegetable oil. Using a ¼-cup measure, scoop the batter onto the warm skillet. Add 6 to 8 blueberries, pressing them gently into each pancake. Cook for 2 to 3 minutes until small bubbles form on the surface of the pancakes, and then flip. Reduce the heat to medium-low and cook on the opposite sides for 1 to 2 minutes, or until golden brown.
5. Transfer the cooked pancakes to a baking sheet and place in a preheated 200°F oven to keep warm. Repeat the process with the remaining batter, adding more butter or vegetable oil to the skillet when needed. Serve immediately.

DRY MIX

1 cup all-purpose flour

2 tablespoons sugar

1 tablespoon baking powder

⅛ teaspoon salt

WET MIX

1 cup ricotta

¾ cup whole milk

1 large egg

1½ teaspoons finely grated lemon zest

½ teaspoon pure vanilla extract

1 tablespoon butter, melted and cooled

ADD IN

1 cup fresh blueberries

Butter or vegetable oil, for the skillet

PRO-TIP

In the summer, I love using fresh blueberries, but in the winter months, I favor frozen wild blueberries. Be sure to let them defrost, and then drain before adding them to the pancakes.

peanut butter and chocolate pancakes

DRY MIX

1 cup all-purpose flour

¼ cup light brown sugar

¼ cup unsweetened cocoa powder

1 tablespoon baking powder

⅛ teaspoon salt

WET MIX

¾ cup plus 2 tablespoons whole milk

¼ cup plus 2 tablespoons creamy peanut butter

1 large egg

1 tablespoon unsalted butter, melted and cooled

Butter or vegetable oil, for the skillet

Makes 8 pancakes

These pancakes are Reese's peanut butter cups in breakfast form. Really, they walk the line between breakfast and dessert. If you wanted to live on the edge, may I recommend serving them with a few scoops of vanilla ice cream?

1. In a medium bowl, mix together the flour, sugar, cocoa powder, baking powder, and salt.

2. In a measuring cup or small bowl, measure out the milk. Add the peanut butter, egg, and melted butter and beat until thoroughly combined.

3. All at once, add the wet ingredients to the dry ingredients and mix until just combined. The batter should have some small to medium lumps.

4. Preheat your skillet over medium heat and brush with 1½ teaspoons of butter or a teaspoon of vegetable oil. Using a ¼-cup measure, scoop the batter onto the warm skillet. Cook for 2 to 3 minutes until small bubbles form on the surface of the pancakes, and then flip. Reduce the heat to medium-low and cook on the opposite sides for 1 to 2 minutes, or until golden brown.

5. Transfer the cooked pancakes to a baking sheet and place in a preheated 200°F oven to keep warm. Repeat the process with the remaining batter, adding more butter or vegetable oil to the skillet when needed. Serve immediately.

chocolate pistachio pancakes }

When I was a kid, I was the weirdo nine-year-old at the ice cream shop that would order pistachio ice cream. Perhaps my taste buds were more advanced than other kids, or maybe I thought the pale green color was just plain pretty. Regardless, I've loved pistachios ever since. In this stack, the pistachios are folded into chocolate pancake goodness to create a throwback that sure is good.

1. In a medium bowl, mix together the flour, cocoa powder, sugar, baking powder, and salt.

2. In a measuring cup or small bowl, measure out the milk. Add the egg, and melted butter and beat until thoroughly combined.

3. All at once, add the wet ingredients to the dry ingredients and mix until just combined. The batter should have some small to medium lumps. Gently fold in the pistachios.

4. Preheat your skillet over medium heat and brush with 1½ teaspoons of butter or a teaspoon of vegetable oil. Using a ¼-cup measure, scoop the batter onto the warm skillet. Cook for 2 to 3 minutes until small bubbles form on the surface of the pancakes, and then flip. Reduce the heat to medium-low and cook on the opposite sides for 1 to 2 minutes, or until golden brown.

5. Transfer the cooked pancakes to a baking sheet and place in a preheated 200°F oven to keep warm. Repeat the process with the remaining batter, adding more butter or vegetable oil to the skillet when needed. Serve immediately.

DRY MIX
¾ cup all-purpose flour

⅓ cup unsweetened Dutch-process cocoa powder

3 tablespoons sugar

1 tablespoon baking powder

¼ teaspoon salt

WET MIX
1¼ cups whole milk

1 large egg

1 tablespoon melted butter, cooled slightly

MIX-IN
¼ cup chopped pistachios

Butter or vegetable oil, for the skillet

summer corn pancakes

Makes 8 pancakes

These pancakes are like a summer dream on a plate. When corn is in abundance, a stack of these is in order. The corn is buttery and sweet, while the cornmeal gives these pancakes heartiness and a toothsome texture. Serve them hot with a dollop of butter, and syrup.

1. In a small skillet, melt the butter over medium heat. Add the corn and sauté for 3 to 5 minutes until lightly browned. Remove from the heat and set aside to cool.
2. In a medium bowl, mix together the flour, cornmeal, sugar, baking powder, and salt.
3. In a measuring cup or small bowl, measure out the milk. Add the egg and vanilla and beat until combined
4. All at once, add the wet ingredients to the dry ingredients and mix until just combined. The batter should have some small to medium lumps. Gently fold in the corn kernels.
5. Preheat your skillet over medium heat and brush with 1½ teaspoons of butter or a teaspoon of vegetable oil. Using a ¼-cup measure, scoop the batter onto the warm skillet. Cook for 2 to 3 minutes until small bubbles form on the surface of the pancakes, and then flip. Reduce the heat to medium-low and cook on the opposite sides for about 1 minute, or until golden brown.
6. Transfer the cooked pancakes to a baking sheet and place in a preheated 200°F oven to keep warm. Repeat the process with the remaining batter, adding more butter or vegetable oil to the skillet when needed. Serve immediately.

CORN

1 tablespoon unsalted butter

1 ear of sweet corn, kernels cut off the cob

DRY MIX

1 cup all-purpose flour

¼ cup cornmeal

1 tablespoon plus 1½ teaspoons sugar

2 teaspoons baking powder

⅛ teaspoon salt

WET MIX

1 cup whole milk

1 large egg

½ teaspoon pure vanilla extract

Butter or vegetable oil, for the skillet

HEADS-UP

If it's winter and you find yourself craving the taste of summer, feel free to use frozen sweet corn in this recipe.

coconut pancakes

DRY MIX

1 cup all-purpose flour

1 tablespoon sugar

1 tablespoon baking powder

¼ teaspoon salt

WET MIX

½ cup coconut milk

¼ cup cream of coconut

1 large egg

1 tablespoon butter, melted and cooled

MIX-IN

¼ cup unsweetened coconut flakes

Butter or vegetable oil, for the skillet

HEADS-UP

Cream of coconut can usually be found in the cocktail mixer section of your grocery store. I usually use the brand Coco Lopez.

Makes 8 pancakes

These pancakes taste exactly how suntan lotion smells. I know I'm not doing a good job at selling these, but trust me they're incredible. The coconut cream works delicious wonders when combined with the coconut milk and coconut flakes. These pancakes are perfect any time, but I think they're especially awesome on a cold winter's morning—one taste and it'll be hard not to imagine you're on a warm, tropical island.

1. In a medium bowl, mix together the flour, sugar, baking powder, and salt.
2. In a measuring cup or small bowl, measure out the coconut milk. Add the cream of coconut, egg, and melted butter and beat until thoroughly combined.
3. All at once, add the wet ingredients to the dry ingredients and mix until just combined. The batter should have some small to medium lumps. Gently fold in the coconut flakes.
4. Preheat your skillet over medium heat and brush with 1½ teaspoons of butter or a teaspoon of vegetable oil. Using a ¼-cup measure, scoop the batter onto the warm skillet. Cook for 2 to 3 minutes until small bubbles form on the surface of the pancakes, and then flip. Reduce the heat to medium-low and cook on the opposite sides for 1 to 2 minutes, or until golden brown.
5. Transfer the cooked pancakes to a baking sheet and place in a preheated 200°F oven to keep warm. Repeat the process with the remaining batter, adding more butter or vegetable oil to the skillet when needed. Serve immediately.

german apple popovers

Think of these as the mini version of the classic German Apple Pancake. The apples are cooked in spices, brown sugar, and butter until tender and then the batter is poured over them. When they come out of the oven, they'll be puffed and golden brown with gorgeous speckles of spiced apples. Pretty perfect for a fall day.

1. Preheat the oven to 350°F. Generously coat a muffin pan with the vegetable oil or spray and set aside.
2. In a small bowl, mix together the brown sugar, cinnamon, nutmeg, and a pinch of salt until combined. Add the apples to the sugar mixture and toss until the apple pieces are thoroughly coated. In a small skillet, melt the butter over medium-low heat. Add the apples and cook until slightly tender, 3 to 5 minutes. Set aside.
3. In a medium bowl, combine the flour, granulated sugar, and salt. In a measuring cup or small bowl, measure out the milk, add the eggs and vanilla, and beat until combined.
4. Pour the wet ingredients into the dry ingredients and mix until nearly smooth. The batter will be thin with a few lumps. If you'd like, you can transfer the batter to a large measuring cup or bowl with a spout; this will make it easier to pour the batter into the muffin wells.
5. Preheat the muffin pan in the oven for 2 to 3 minutes. Remove it from the oven and add a teaspoon of sautéed apples to each well. Carefully pour the batter on top, filling the wells a little more than halfway. Bake for 30 to 35 minutes, until tall, puffed, and golden brown. Serve immediately.

Vegetable oil or cooking spray for the muffin pan

SAUTÉED APPLES

1 tablespoon light brown sugar

½ teaspoon ground cinnamon

⅛ teaspoon freshly grated nutmeg

1 medium apple, peeled, cored, and diced

Salt

1 tablespoon unsalted butter

BATTER

1 ½ cups all-purpose flour

3 tablespoons granulated sugar

⅛ teaspoon salt

1½ cups whole milk, at room temperature

3 large eggs, at room temperature

1 teaspoon pure vanilla extract

banana bourbon pancakes }

Makes 8 pancakes

These pancakes are killer. They start with sliced bananas gently sautéed with butter, brown sugar, bourbon, and a dash of cinnamon. The bourbon-enhanced bananas will caramelize, adding a bold and distinctive flavor to these pancakes. The only thing that could send them over the moon is topping them with a generous pour of Bourbon Maple Syrup (page 153).

1. In a small skillet, melt the butter over medium heat. Add the bananas, sugar, bourbon, cinnamon and toss lightly until bananas are evenly coated. Sauté for 2 to 3 minutes until the bananas are lightly browned. Remove from the heat and set aside to cool.

2. In a medium bowl, mix together the flour, sugar, baking powder, baking soda, and salt.

3. In a measuring cup or small bowl, measure out the buttermilk. Add the egg, bourbon, melted butter, and vanilla and beat until thoroughly combined.

4. All at once, add the wet ingredients to the dry ingredients and mix until just combined. The batter should have some small to medium lumps.

5. Preheat your skillet over medium heat and brush with 1½ teaspoons of butter or a teaspoon of vegetable oil. Using a ¼-cup measure, scoop the batter onto the warm skillet. Add 4 to 5 slices of banana to each pancake, pressing them in lightly. Cook for 2 to 3 minutes until small bubbles form on the surface of the pancakes, and then flip. Reduce the heat to medium-low and cook on the opposite sides for 1 to 2 minutes, or until golden brown.

6. Transfer the cooked pancakes to a baking sheet and place in a preheated 200°F oven to keep warm. Repeat the process with the remaining batter, adding more butter or vegetable oil to the skillet when needed. Serve immediately with warm bourbon maple syrup, if you like.

BANANAS

1½ teaspoons unsalted butter

2 ripe bananas, thinly sliced

1 tablespoon light brown sugar

1 tablespoon bourbon

½ teaspoon ground cinnamon

DRY MIX

1 cup all-purpose flour

2 tablespoons light brown sugar

1 teaspoon baking powder

1 teaspoon baking soda

¼ teaspoon salt

WET MIX

¾ cup buttermilk, plus 2 tablespoons, shaken

1 large egg

2 tablespoons bourbon

1½ teaspoons melted butter, cooled

½ teaspoon pure vanilla extract

Butter or vegetable oil, for the skillet

Bourbon Maple Syrup, for serving (optional)

cinnamon-sugar popovers

Vegetable oil or cooking spray for the muffin pan

BATTER

1½ cups all-purpose flour

3 tablespoons granulated sugar

1 tablespoon ground cinnamon

¼ teaspoon salt

1½ cups whole milk, at room temperature

3 large eggs, at room temperature

TOPPING

1 tablespoon unsalted butter, at room temperature

1 teaspoon ground cinnamon

2 tablespoons sugar

Makes 12 popovers

These popovers are inspired by one of my favorite snacks: buttery cinnamon-sugar toast. The batter has a good amount of sugar and cinnamon, and once the popovers exit the oven, they are quickly brushed with butter and topped with a liberal amount of cinnamon sugar. I enjoy these custardy puffs alongside a cup of strong coffee.

1. Preheat the oven to 350°F. Generously coat a muffin pan with the vegetable oil or spray and set aside.

2. In a medium bowl, combine the flour, sugar, cinnamon, and salt. Measure out the milk. In a measuring cup or small bowl, add the eggs and beat until combined.

3. Pour the wet ingredients into the dry ingredients and mix until nearly smooth. The batter will be thin with a few lumps. If you'd like, you can transfer the batter to a large measuring cup or bowl with a spout; this will make it easier to pour the batter into the muffin wells.

4. Preheat the muffin pan in the oven for 2 to 3 minutes. Carefully pour the batter in each well, filling them about halfway. Bake for 30 to 35 minutes until tall, puffed, and golden brown.

5. While the popovers are baking, prepare the cinnamon-sugar topping. Melt the 1 tablespoon of butter and set aside. In a small bowl, mix together the cinnamon and sugar. Brush each baked popover with a light coating of butter, then sprinkle the cinnamon-sugar over the entire batch. Serve immediately.

oatmeal pancakes

Makes 8 pancakes

If when you wake, you look forward to a bowl of warm, spice-laden oatmeal, then these pancakes were designed for you. I, on the other hand, am not an oatmeal person—it's a texture thing, guys. I do, though, love oatmeal rolled into baked goods. Oat flour and rolled oats give these pancakes an awesome wholesome quality. Feel free to top them with fresh fruit and rich maple syrup.

1. In a medium bowl, mix together the flour, oat flour, sugar, cinnamon, baking powder, and salt.

2. In a measuring cup or small bowl, measure out the milk. Add the egg and vanilla and beat until thoroughly combined.

3. All at once, add the wet ingredients to the dry ingredients and mix until just combined. The batter should have some small to medium lumps. Gently fold in the rolled oats.

4. Preheat your skillet over medium heat and brush with 1½ teaspoons of butter or a teaspoon of vegetable oil. Using a ¼-cup measure, scoop the batter onto the warm skillet. Cook for 2 to 3 minutes until small bubbles form on the surface of the pancakes, and then flip. Reduce the heat to medium-low and cook on the opposite sides for 1 to 2 minutes, or until golden brown.

5. Transfer the cooked pancakes to a baking sheet and place in a preheated 200°F oven to keep warm. Repeat the process with the remaining batter, adding more butter or vegetable oil to the skillet when needed. Serve immediately.

DRY MIX

1 cup all-purpose flour

¼ cup oat flour

2 tablespoons light brown sugar

2 teaspoons ground cinnamon

1½ teaspoons baking powder

⅛ teaspoon salt

WET MIX

1 cup whole milk

1 large egg

1 teaspoon pure vanilla extract

MIX-IN

¼ cup rolled oats

Butter or vegetable oil, for the skillet

PRO-TIP

You can find oat flour at most grocery stores, or you can make your own. To do so, add rolled oats to a food processor and pulse until finely ground.

multigrain pancakes

Los Angeles has some great hiking spots—and I've become a fan of exploring them. On the weekends, I love waking up (a little!) early and making these pancakes, preworkout. They're loaded with nutrients—but still light and fluffy. They give me all the fuel I need to make that long trek up an L.A. version of a mountain.

1. In a medium bowl, mix together the flours, baking powder, and salt.

2. In a measuring cup or small bowl, measure out the almond milk. Add the egg, agave, and vanilla and beat until thoroughly combined.

3. All at once, add the wet ingredients to the dry ingredients and mix until just combined. The batter should have some small to medium lumps. Gently fold in the rolled oats.

4. Preheat your skillet over medium heat and brush with 1½ teaspoons of butter or a teaspoon of vegetable oil. Using a ¼-cup measure, scoop the batter onto the warm skillet. Cook for 2 to 3 minutes until small bubbles form on the surface of the pancakes, and then flip. Reduce the heat to medium-low and cook on the opposite sides for 1 to 2 minutes, or until golden brown.

5. Transfer the cooked pancakes to a baking sheet and place in a preheated 200°F oven to keep warm. Repeat the process with the remaining batter, adding more butter or vegetable oil to the skillet when needed. Serve immediately.

DRY MIX

½ cup all-purpose flour

¼ cup whole-wheat flour

¼ cup rye flour

1½ tablespoons baking powder

¼ teaspoon salt

WET MIX

¾ cup almond milk

1 large egg

2 tablespoons agave nectar

1 teaspoon pure vanilla extract

Butter or vegetable oil, for the skillet

lemon cloud pancakes

Makes 8 pancakes

These pancakes taste like a cloud. I know that's an unreasonable promise, but they do. They're light as a feather—thanks to the whipped egg whites gently folded in—a technique you're more than welcome to implement in other pancake recipes. The cottage cheese adds an awesome creaminess and the abundance of fresh lemon flavor adds a punch of brightness.

1. In a medium bowl, mix together the flour, sugar, salt, and lemon zest.
2. In a small bowl, beat together the cottage cheese, lemon juice, egg yolks, and melted butter until thoroughly combined.
3. All at once, add the wet ingredients to the dry ingredients and mix until just combined.
4. Using a hand mixer, whip the egg whites until they reach medium peaks, about 5 minutes. Gently fold the egg whites into the batter until thoroughly combined.
5. Preheat your skillet over medium heat and brush with 1½ teaspoons of butter or a teaspoon of vegetable oil. Using a ¼-cup measure, scoop the batter onto the warm skillet. Cook for 2 to 3 minutes until small bubbles form on the surface of the pancakes, and then flip. Reduce the heat to medium-low and cook on the opposite sides for 1 to 2 minutes, or until golden brown.
6. Transfer the cooked pancakes to a baking sheet and place in a preheated 200°F oven to keep warm. Repeat the process with the remaining batter, adding more butter or vegetable oil to the skillet when needed. Serve immediately.

DRY MIX

½ cup all-purpose flour

2 tablespoons sugar

¼ teaspoon salt

1 tablespoon finely grated lemon zest

WET MIX

¾ cup full-fat cottage cheese

2 tablespoons freshly squeezed lemon juice

2 large eggs, separated

1 tablespoon unsalted butter, melted and cooled

Butter or vegetable oil, for the skillet

strawberries and cream crêpe cake

PASTRY CREAM

1 tablespoon all-
purpose flour

1 tablespoon
cornstarch

1 cup whole milk, plus
1 tablespoon

1 teaspoon pure
vanilla extract

2 large egg yolks

3 tablespoons
granulated sugar

¼ cup heavy cream

1 tablespoon
confectioners' sugar,
sifted

1 pound fresh
strawberries, thinly
and evenly sliced
horizontally

Makes 1 cream crêpe cake

As a lifelong tennis fan, I've always dreamed of attending Wimbledon. While I'd be so stoked to watch tennis played on grass, I'd really have my heart set on eating a big bowl of their famous strawberries and cream. This crêpe is an ode to Wimbledon. I'm not going to lie, it's a little labor-intensive. In between the crêpes is a thick layer of rich pastry cream and fresh strawberries. After assembling, chill the cake in the refrigerator to make it easy to slice.

1. In a small bowl, sift together the flour and cornstarch. Set aside. In a small saucepan, set over medium-heat, combine the milk and vanilla and bring to a boil, then immediately remove from the heat.
2. In a medium bowl, whisk together the egg yolks and granulated sugar until the mixture is a pale yellow. Add the flour mixture and whisk until completely smooth. While whisking the egg mixture, simultaneously add about half of the milk to the bowl. Slowly adding the hot milk to the egg mixture will prevent the eggs from scrambling. Transfer the custard to the saucepan and place over medium-high heat. Bring it to a boil, whisking the entire time, being sure to scrape the bottom and edges of the pan. Lower the heat and cook until the custard has thickened, 2 to 3 minutes. Remove the pastry cream from the heat and pour through a sieve into a bowl. This will eliminate any lumps. Press a piece of plastic wrap directly onto the cream's surface so it doesn't form a skin, and transfer it to the refrigerator to chill for 1 hour.
3. Combine the heavy cream and confectioners' sugar in a medium bowl. Using a hand mixer beat until firm peaks form. Remove chilled pastry cream from the refrigerator and gently fold the whipped cream into the pastry cream. Return the lightened pastry cream to the refrigerator until you're ready to assemble the crêpe cake.

4. To the jar of a blender, add the eggs, milk, water, and melted butter and pulse for a few seconds until the liquids are combined. Add the flour, granulated sugar, and salt. Pulse for 10 seconds or so until the flour is incorporated, being careful not to overblend. Transfer the batter to a bowl and cover with plastic wrap. Place the batter in the refrigerator for an hour to rest.

5. Place a crêpe pan, or nonstick skillet, over medium heat. Brush the skillet with a very light coating of butter. Add ¼ cup of batter to the center of the pan and swirl it around until the bottom is coated evenly. Cook until the edges of the crêpe pull away from the pan, 1 to 2 minutes. Flip and cook on the opposite side for another 30 seconds. Repeat the process with the batter to make a total of 8 crêpes. Stack the crêpes and allow them to cool to room temperature before assembling the cake.

6. To assemble the cake: Gather your crêpes, pastry cream, and sliced strawberries. Start by layering two crêpes on a piece of parchment paper placed on a serving plate. Add a heaping tablespoon of pastry cream on top of the first crêpe, spreading it evenly. Add an even layer of strawberries. Top with another crêpe and repeat the layering until you've used all of the pastry cream and strawberries. When completed you should have about 6 layers. Transfer the crêpe cake to the refrigerator to chill for at least 30 minutes before slicing and serving.

CRÊPE BATTER

2 large eggs

1 cup whole milk

¼ cup water

2 tablespoons unsalted butter, melted and cooled

1 cup all-purpose flour

2 tablespoons granulated sugar

⅛ teaspoon salt

Butter for the crêpe pan

DINNER
PANCAKES

As a kid, dinner was always a big deal. My mother, despite being strapped for time, would always whip up something for us to eat together. It was time for us to reconvene and hash out the details and happenings of our day. Now that I'm somewhat of a grown-up, I admittedly don't take it as seriously as I should. (There are many nights where it's just me and a bowl of cereal in front of the TV.) But whenever I do take the time to make a proper dinner, I always turn to the recipes that follow. Some are simple and can be made in a mere fifteen minutes, while others require a bit more time, but all are delicious, comforting, and a highlight to the end of your day.

jalapeño corn cakes

DRY MIX

1 cup all-purpose flour

2 tablespoons cornmeal

1 teaspoon baking powder

1 teaspoon baking soda

⅛ teaspoon kosher salt

WET MIX

1 cup buttermilk, plus 2 tablespoons, shaken

1 large egg

MIX-INS

1 ear of corn, kernels sliced off the cob

½ jalapeño pepper, seeded and diced

½ red bell pepper, seeded and diced

½ cup Monterey Jack cheese, grated

Butter or vegetable oil, for the skillet

Avocado butter (page 155), for serving (optional)

Makes 8 corn cakes

The summers in Los Angeles—and almost anywhere, really mean gorgeous, bountiful amounts of corn. These pancakes, while fluffy and tall, have a crunchy texture thanks to cornmeal, red bell peppers, and fresh corn. The Monterey Jack gives it a good cheesiness, though I'd bet other good melting cheeses like fontina, mozzarella, or cheddar would do well here, too.

1. In a medium bowl, mix together the flour, cornmeal, baking powder, baking soda, and salt.

2. In a measuring cup, or small bowl, measure out the buttermilk. Add the egg and beat until thoroughly combined.

3. All at once, add the wet ingredients to the dry ingredients and mix until just combined. The batter should have some small to medium lumps. Gently fold in the corn kernels, jalapeño, bell pepper, and cheese.

4. Preheat your skillet over medium heat and brush with 1½ teaspoons of butter or a teaspoon of vegetable oil. Using ¼-cup measure, scoop the batter onto the warm skillet. Cook for 2 to 3 minutes until small bubbles form on the surface of the pancakes, and then flip. Reduce the heat to medium-low and cook on the opposite sides for 1 to 2 minutes, or until golden brown.

5. Transfer the cooked pancakes to a baking sheet and place in a preheated 200°F oven to keep warm. Repeat the process with the remaining batter, adding more butter or vegetable oil to the skillet when needed. Serve immediately.

smoked gouda sweet potato latkes }

Makes 16 latkes

Ingredients:

1 pound sweet potatoes, peeled

1 teaspoon kosher salt

1 shallot, minced

¼ cup all-purpose flour

2 large eggs

¼ teaspoon freshly ground black pepper

¾ cup smoked gouda, finely grated

Vegetable oil, for the skillet

Apple sauce, for serving (optional)

GLUTEN-FREE

Smoked gouda has a pretty special place in my heart. Unlike a lot of cheeses that are smoked, this one gets a traditional smoke (versus a cold smoke) that's similar to bacon, in a large brick oven over hickory embers. The flavor is pronounced and complements the sweet sweet potato nicely.

1. Using a hand grater, coarsely grate the sweet potatoes, lengthwise. Transfer the potatoes to a bowl, sprinkle with ¼ teaspoon of kosher salt, and let stand for 5 minutes. Gather the potatoes in the center of a few layers of cheesecloth and squeeze out the excess water.

2. Place the potatoes into a medium bowl, along with the shallots, flour, eggs, ¾ teaspoon of salt, pepper, and smoked gouda. Mix until thoroughly combined.

3. Place a skillet over medium-high heat, and pour in vegetable oil until it reaches ½ inch up the sides. Once the oil is hot, for each latke, place a heaping tablespoon of the potato mixture into the pan, slightly flattening the latke with the back of the spoon. Cook the latkes on their first side for about a minute or two or until golden brown. Carefully flip and cook on the opposite sides for an additional minute. Transfer to paper towels to drain and then place them in a preheated 200°F oven to keep warm. Repeat the process with the remaining potato mixture. Serve immediately.

goat cheese quinoa cakes

1 cup quinoa

1¾ cups water

1 cup panko bread crumbs

3 large eggs, beaten

4 ounces goat cheese, crumbled

2 garlic cloves, minced

½ shallot, minced

1½ tablespoons olive oil

1 tablespoon fresh chives, minced

¾ teaspoon salt

Vegetable oil, for the skillet

Makes 11 cakes

Cheese, at first, might seem like an odd combination with this superfood, but it's a win of a marriage. I hadn't thought to pair quinoa with cheese until I was in line at the grocery store and someone inquired about the random items in my basket, "You're mixing quinoa with goat cheese?" Though I'd obviously not intended to combine the two, I replied, "Uhh . . . why, yes. Yes I am."

1. Thoroughly rinse the quinoa in a sieve. Add the water and the clean quinoa to a medium saucepan and place over medium-high heat. Bring the mixture to a boil, cover pot, and cook for 15 to 17 minutes until the liquid is absorbed. Set aside and allow to cool completely, about 20 minutes.

2. In a large bowl, mix together the cooled quinoa, bread crumbs, eggs, goat cheese, garlic, shallot, olive oil, chives, and salt until thoroughly combined. Cover with plastic wrap and refrigerate for 30 minutes.

3. Scoop 2 tablespoons of the chilled quinoa mixture onto the palm of your hand. Form into a patty that is 3 inches in diameter and about 1 inch thick. Continue to make patties with the remaining mixture.

4. Place a skillet over medium-high heat, and pour in vegetable oil until it reaches ¼ inch up the sides. Once the oil is hot, carefully add the patties, being sure to not overcrowd the pan. Cook for 2 to 3 minutes until golden brown. Gently flip and cook on opposite sides for a minute or two. Transfer to paper towels to drain and then place them in a preheated 200°F oven to keep warm. Repeat the process to cook the remaining cakes. Serve immediately.

spicy black bean cakes

1 tablespoon olive oil

¼ cup red bell pepper, seeded and diced

½ cup yellow corn kernels (canned, frozen, or fresh)

1 jalapeño pepper, seeded and minced

2 teaspoons ground cumin

1 garlic clove, minced

One 15-ounce can black beans, rinsed and drained well

½ cup cornmeal

1 large egg, lightly beaten

2 tablespoons fresh cilantro, minced

2 teaspoons hot sauce

¾ teaspoon salt

Vegetable oil, for the skillet

Avocado butter (page 155), for serving

PRO-TIP

My favorite Mexican hot sauce is Tapatío.

GLUTEN-FREE

Makes 6 cakes

I came up with this recipe one night when I was watching my favorite television series of all time, *Friday Night Lights*. I was craving something with a spicy Texan flair, yet I only had frozen corn and a can of black beans in my pantry. I loved them so much that I remade them adding diced red bell pepper and fresh cilantro. These work great as a side dish or as a main course. I love smearing them with some avocado butter, and eating them accompanied by a cold beer while watching Coach Taylor give a dramatic speech. Texas forever!

1. In a medium skillet over moderately high heat, heat the olive oil. When the oil is hot, add the bell pepper, corn kernels, jalapeño, and cumin and mix together. Cook for 2 to 3 minutes until the vegetables become translucent. Add the garlic on top of vegetable mixture and cook until fragrant, about 1 minute more.

2. In a medium bowl, using a fork, smash the black beans. Add the warm vegetable mixture, cornmeal, egg, cilantro, hot sauce, and salt and mix until thoroughly combined. Cover with plastic wrap and refrigerate for 30 minutes.

3. Scoop ¼ cup of the black bean mixture onto the palm of your hand. Form into a patty that is 3 inches in diameter and about 1 inch thick. Continue to make patties with the remaining mixture.

4. Place a skillet over medium-high heat, and pour in vegetable oil until it reaches ¼ inch up the sides. Once the oil is hot, carefully add the patties, being sure not to overcrowd the pan. Cook for 2 to 3 minutes until golden brown. Gently flip and cook on the opposite sides for a minute or two. Transfer to paper towels to drain and then place them in a preheated 200°F oven to keep warm. Repeat the process to cook the remaining cakes. Serve immediately.

goat cheese and grits cakes

4 cups whole milk

1 cup water

2 tablespoons un-salted butter

2¼ cups stone-ground corn grits

½ cup goat cheese, crumbled

2 teaspoons salt

Vegetable oil, for the skillet

GLUTEN-FREE

Makes 12 cakes

I've been in love with cheesy grits from the start. My mother was unfamiliar with how to make them, and when I was growing up she used to just buy the instant packets to shut me up. It wasn't until I moved to North Carolina for college that I fell in love with the real, stone-ground grits. These cakes start with a big batch of grits cooked on the stovetop, which is then put in the refrigerator to firm. Once firm, they're cut into rounds and pan fried until they develop a crispy crust on both sides. I love using them as a crunchy base for soft braised meat with gravy or a runny, poached egg. And be sure to save the scraps! They're perfect for breakfast the next morning, smothered in jam.

1. In a large pot, bring the milk, water, and butter to a boil. Gradually whisk in the corn grits. Reduce the heat to low and cook, stirring the entire time, until the grits are thick and start to pull away from the sides of the pot, 2 to 3 minutes. Remove from the heat.

2. Stir in the goat cheese and salt. Taste and add more salt, if you like. Transfer the grits mixture to a greased baking sheet and spread it out evenly and compactly to a ¾-inch thickness. Wrap with plastic wrap and transfer to the refrigerator for an hour until cool and firm.

3. Using a 3-inch biscuit or cookie cutter, cut out the grit cakes. Place a cast-iron skillet over medium-high heat, and pour in vegetable oil until it reaches 1 inch up the sides. Once oil is hot, carefully add the cakes to the pan and cook for 1 to 2 minutes until golden brown. Gently flip and cook on the opposite sides for 1 to 2 minutes more. Transfer to paper towels to drain and then place them in a preheated 200°F oven to keep warm. Repeat the process to cook the remaining cakes. Serve immediately.

falafel cakes

Two 15-ounce cans chickpeas, rinsed and drained

4 garlic cloves

1 shallot

½ cup packed fresh flat-leaf parsley leaves

2 teaspoon ground cumin

½ teaspoon cayenne pepper

1 tablespoon freshly, squeezed lemon juice

1 teaspoon baking soda

1 teaspoon salt

½ cup plus 1 tablespoon dry bread crumbs

2 large eggs

Vegetable oil, for the skillet

GLUTEN-FREE

Makes 12 cakes

In my street food dreams, I'm usually eating crispy, fried falafel balls sandwiched in warm pita bread. When you pair these falafel cakes with a fresh, lemon-kissed tomato salad and a few slices of pita bread, this walk-'n-talk snack transforms into a filling, vegetarian dinner that's totally worthy of a knife, fork, and a tall glass of chilled wine.

1. To the bowl of a food processor, add half of the chickpeas and pulse until roughly chopped. Transfer to a large bowl. Place the second half of chickpeas in the food processor with the garlic, shallot, parsley, cumin, cayenne, lemon juice, baking soda, and salt. Pulse until it becomes thick, 20 to 30 seconds.

2. Transfer the mixture to the bowl with the chopped chickpeas. Mix in the bread crumbs and egg. Cover with plastic wrap and refrigerate for 30 minutes.

3. Scoop 2 tablespoons of the chickpea mixture onto the palm of your hand. Form into a patty that is 3 inches in diameter and about 1 inch thick. Continue to make patties with the remaining mixture.

4. Place a skillet over medium-high heat, and pour in vegetable oil until it reaches ½ inch up the sides. Once the oil is hot, carefully add the patties, being sure to not overcrowd the pan. Cook for 2 to 3 minutes until golden brown. Gently flip and cook on the opposite sides for 1 to 2 minutes. Transfer to paper towels to drain and then place them in a preheated 200°F oven to keep warm. Repeat the process to cook the remaining cakes. Serve immediately.

sour cream and chive potato latkes

Makes 16 latkes

Latkes are a staple around the holidays. I'm a strong advocate for them anytime of the year. When done right, the edges are brittle, golden brown, both sides crispy, and the center's soft. The sour cream gives these latkes an extra creaminess I love, and the chives give them a nice freshness.

1. Using a hand grater, coarsely grate the potatoes, lengthwise. Transfer the potatoes to a bowl, sprinkle with ¼ teaspoon of kosher salt and let stand for 5 minutes. Gather the potatoes in the center of a few layers of cheesecloth and squeeze out the excess water.

2. Place the potatoes into a bowl, along with the shallot, garlic, egg, sour cream, chives, pepper, and ½ teaspoon of salt. Mix until thoroughly combined.

3. Place a skillet over medium-high heat, and pour in vegetable oil until it reaches ½ inch up the sides. Once the oil is hot, for each latke place a heaping teaspoon of the potato mixture into the skillet, flattening it slightly with the back of the spoon. Cook for a minute or two until golden brown. Carefully flip and cook on the opposite side for 1 minute more. Transfer to paper towels to drain and then place them in a warm oven. Repeat the process to make the remaining latkes. Serve immediately.

1 pound of russet potatoes, peeled

¾ teaspoon kosher salt

1 shallot, minced

1 garlic clove, minced

1 large egg, beaten

1 cup sour cream

¼ cup fresh chives, minced

¼ teaspoon freshly ground black pepper

Vegetable oil, for the skillet

Apple sauce, for serving (optional)

GLUTEN-FREE

salmon cakes with spicy tartar sauce

SALMON CAKES

1 pound boneless salmon fillet

Olive oil

Salt

Freshly ground black pepper

1 shallot, minced

1 garlic clove, minced

1 large egg

1 cup plus 2 tablespoons dry bread crumbs

1 tablespoon fresh Italian parsley, chopped

2 teaspoons Dijon mustard

1 teaspoon Old Bay Seasoning

½ teaspoon hot sauce (Tapatío)

1 tablespoon freshly squeezed lemon juice

½ teaspoon finely grated lemon zest

Vegetable oil, for the skillet

Makes 10 cakes

I'm sort of embarrassed to admit this, but I was terrified of gaining the cliché "freshmen 15" in my first year of college. To make sure this didn't happen, I started a healthy eating regimen. I quickly became obsessed with salmon, and since I was sans kitchen, I mastered cooking salmon in the microwave—a technique I'm still very proud of. It wasn't until I moved into my first real apartment that I found broiling salmon to be the way to go—it's nearly fool-proof. These cakes are definitely a step up from the bland salmon of my college days. They're bright, fresh, and really flavorful, making them perfect for an easy, light dinner.

1. Preheat the oven to 350°F. Coat the salmon evenly with a teaspoon of olive oil and a pinch of salt and pepper. Place the salmon on a parchment paper–lined baking sheet, skin side down, and roast until cooked through, 8 to 10 minutes. Allow the salmon to cool to room temperature.

2. In a small sauté pan, over medium heat, add a teaspoon of olive oil. When oil is hot, add the minced shallot and cook until translucent, 2 to 3 minutes. Add garlic and cook until fragant, about 1 minute. Take pan off heat and set aside.

3. Using a fork, flake the salmon into a medium bowl. Add the bread crumbs, cooked shallot mixture, egg, Italian parsley, Dijon mustard, Old Bay Seasoning, hot sauce, lemon juice, and the lemon zest. Mix it all together until thoroughly combined. Cover the bowl with plastic wrap and transfer to the refrigerator to chill for an hour.

SPICY TARTAR SAUCE

½ cup mayonnaise

1 teaspoon freshly squeezed lemon juice

½ teaspoon Dijon mustard

3 cornichons, diced

⅛ teaspoon Sriracha sauce

1 tablespoon jalapeño pepper, seeded and finely chopped

4. Scoop 3 tablespoons of the salmon mixture onto the palm of your hand. Form into a patty, about 3 inches in diameter and ½ inch thick. Repeat the process with the remaining mixture.

5. Place a cast-iron skillet over medium-high heat, and pour in vegetable oil until it reaches ¼ inch up the sides. Once the oil is hot, carefully add salmon cakes to the skillet and cook for 2 to 3 minutes until golden brown. Gently flip and cook on the opposite sides for 1 to 2 minutes more. Transfer the salmon cakes to paper towels to drain and then place them in a preheated 200°F oven to keep warm. Repeat the process to cook the remaining cakes. Serve immediately with tartar sauce.

6. To make the spicy tartar sauce: In a small bowl, mix all of the ingredients together until combined. Season with salt to taste.

PRO-TIP

When buying salmon, I always request the center cut. I try my best to buy wild salmon—it's more sustainable and more flavorful. If you're worried about bones, don't hesitate to ask the fishmonger to take out the pinbones.

fried mac 'n cheese cakes

Kosher salt

1 pound elbow macaroni

6 tablespoons unsalted butter

2/3 cup all-purpose flour

3 cups whole milk

3 cups Gruyère cheese, grated

1½ cups sharp cheddar cheese, grated

½ teaspoon freshly ground black pepper

¼ teaspoon freshly grated nutmeg

1½ teaspoons salt

1½ cups bread crumbs

Vegetable oil, for the skillet

Makes 10 cakes

I don't even remember when I first had a fried mac 'n cheese ball; probably because the room stopped and nothing else mattered in the world. Cheesy pasta goodness—and fried? Yes please! I decided to take that notable memory, run with it, and turn it into dinner. With a bigger shape and new form, these Fried Mac 'n Cheese Cakes are ideal for one of those nights when you need a hug in the form of cheese and pasta.

1. Spray a baking sheet with nonstick cooking spray and set aside. Bring a medium pot of salted water to a boil over high heat. Cook the macaroni according to the package directions, 6 to 8 minutes. Drain.

2. In a medium pot, over medium-low heat, melt the butter. Add the flour, mix with the melted butter, and cook for 2 minutes, until the mixture comes together and begins to bubble slightly. Reduce the heat to medium, and while whisking vigorously, pour in the milk. Cook for 1 to 2 minutes, until the sauce becomes thick and smooth. Remove the pan from the heat and fold in the Gruyére, cheddar, pepper, nutmeg, and salt.

3. Gently mix the cooked macaroni into the pot of cheesy sauce. Transfer the sauced macaroni to the lightly greased baking sheet, spreading it evenly and compactly to a ¾-inch thickness. Wrap with plastic wrap and transfer to the refrigerator for 2 hours, or until cool and firm.

4. Using a 3 inch biscuit or cookie cutter, cut out macaroni rounds. Dip the macaroni cakes in the bread crumbs, being sure to evenly coat both sides.

5. Place a cast-iron skillet over medium-high heat, and pour in vegetable oil until it reaches ½ inch up the sides. Once the oil is hot, carefully add the macaroni cakes to the skillet and cook for 1 to 2 minutes until golden brown. Gently flip and cook on the opposite sides for 1 to 2 minutes more. Transfer to paper towels to drain and then place them in a preheated 200°F oven to keep warm. Repeat the process to cook the remaining cakes. Serve immediately.

cheese and sage pancakes

DRY MIX

1 cup all-purpose flour

1 tablespoon baking powder

¼ teaspoon salt

WET MIX

1 cup whole milk

1 large egg

1½ teaspoons unsalted butter, melted and cooled

MIX-INS

2 tablespoons fresh sage, minced

½ cup fontina cheese, finely grated

Butter or vegetable oil, for the skillet

Makes 8 pancakes

The day or two after Thanksgiving might be my favorite food time of the year. The abundance of random leftovers always presents an entertaining challenge of mixing and matching dishes with scrap ingredients. I first made these pancakes with some leftover, almost wilted, sage. The green sage speckles give these pancakes a wintery, cozy feel while the fontina give the centers a cheesiness that makes them pretty great regardless of your fridge's leftover situation.

1. In a medium bowl, mix together the flour, baking powder, and salt.

2. In a measuring cup or small bowl, measure out the milk. Add the egg and melted butter and beat until thoroughly combined.

3. All at once, add the wet ingredients to the dry ingredients and mix until just combined. The batter should have some small to medium lumps. Gently fold in the minced sage and grated cheese.

4. Preheat your cast-iron skillet over medium heat and brush with 1½ teaspoons of butter. Using a ¼-cup measure, scoop the batter onto the warm skillet. Cook for 2 to 3 minutes until small bubbles form on the surface of the pancakes, and then flip. Reduce the heat to medium-low and cook on the opposite sides for 1 to 2 minutes, or until golden brown.

5. Transfer the cooked pancakes to a baking sheet and place them in a preheated 200°F oven to keep warm. Repeat the process to make the remaining cakes. Serve immediately.

olive oil–italian sausage pancakes

I don't think anyone on this planet thought to put olive oil in a pancake until José Andrés did it with his famous recipe for Olive Oil Chocolate Chip Pancakes. I took his idea and turned it savory by swapping out chocolate for spicy Italian sausage. Do right by this pancakes and use a good-quality, extra-virgin olive oil—it will make all the difference.

1. In a medium bowl, mix together the flour, cornmeal, sugar, baking powder, baking soda, and salt.

2. In a measuring cup or small bowl, measure out the buttermilk. Add the egg and olive oil and beat until thoroughly combined.

3. All at once, add the wet ingredients to the dry ingredients and mix until just combined. The batter should have some small to medium lumps. Gently fold in the crumbled, cooked sausage.

4. Preheat your skillet over medium heat and brush with a teaspoon of vegetable oil. Using a ¼-cup measure, scoop the batter onto the warm skillet. Cook for 2 to 3 minutes until small bubbles form on the surface of the pancakes, and then flip. Reduce the heat to medium-low and cook on the opposite sides for 1 to 2 minutes, or until golden brown.

5. Transfer the cooked pancakes to a baking sheet and place in a preheated 200°F oven to keep warm. Repeat the process with the remaining batter. Serve immediately.

DRY MIX

¾ cup all-purpose flour

¼ cup cornmeal

1 tablespoon sugar

1 teaspoon baking powder

1 teaspoon baking soda

⅛ teaspoon salt

WET MIX

1 cup buttermilk, shaken

1 large egg

¼ cup good-quality, extra-virgin olive oil

MIX-INS

¼ cup crumbled spicy Italian sausage, cooked

Vegetable oil, for the skillet

parmesan-mushroom risotto cakes

2 tablespoons olive oil

2 cups cremini mushrooms, sliced

¼ cup shallots, minced

1 cup Arborio rice

2 cups low-sodium chicken broth

½ cup dry white wine

Salt

1 cup Parmigiano-Reggiano, grated

½ cup plain yogurt

2 large eggs

¼ teaspoon crushed red pepper flakes

Vegetable oil, for the skillet

The first time I attempted to make risotto I cried. It was Christmas, the house was full of family and they were all incredibly excited about this risotto I'd talked up. After a few critical mistakes, I ended up with a pot of gummy, dry mess. I stayed away from it for years after that incident, until finally I found the courage to give it another crack. It definitely took a few more tries to get it right, but I found the trick to be that you cannot leave it unattended—something I'm still not very good at accepting, since I have a fondness with multitasking in the kitchen. Luckily you don't have to do that with these risotto cakes. Since we're mixing them with cheese and mushrooms and finishing them with a panfry, it's slightly more forgiving. The crunchy exterior with the creamy, earthy interior—and all sans risotto stress, which is a definite win in my eyes.

1. In a medium pot, heat the olive oil, over medium heat. Add the mushrooms and cook until softened, about 5 to 7 minutes. Add the shallots and cook until translucent, about 3 minutes. Add the Arborio rice, stir in the chicken broth, white wine, and ½ teaspoon of salt and cook for 25 minutes. The liquid will be absorbed, yet the risotto will still be moist and cooked all the way through. Remove the risotto from the pot and place in the refrigerator until cool, about 30 minutes.
2. In a large bowl, whisk together the cheese, yogurt, eggs, pepper flakes, and ½ teaspoon of salt. Add the cooled rice and mix until thoroughly combined. Cover the bowl with plastic wrap and refrigerate for an hour, or until mixture is firm.
3. Scoop 2 tablespoons of the risotto mixture onto the palm of your hand. Form into a cake that is 3 inches in diameter and 1 inch thick. Continue to make cakes, with the remaining mixture.

4. Place a skillet over medium-high heat, and pour in vegetable oil until it reaches 1 inch up the sides. Once the oil is hot, carefully add the cakes, being sure not to overcrowd the skillet. Cook for 2 to 3 minutes until golden brown. Gently flip and cook on the opposite sides for a minute or two. Transfer to paper towels to drain and then place them in a preheated 200°F oven to keep warm. Repeat the process to cook the remaining cakes. Serve immediately.

empera's arepas

1 cup warm water

1 tablespoon unsalted butter, melted

½ teaspoon salt

1 cup precooked white corn meal

½ cup mozzarella cheese, finely grated

Vegetable oil, for the skillet

GLUTEN-FREE

PRO-TIP

Latin markets usually have precooked corn flour. The brand that I'm most familiar with is called Harina P.A.N.

Makes about 8 arepas

In my family I am rarely given jewelry as family heirlooms; instead, I am given recipes. This one was given to me by my aunt Empera who lives in Bogota, Colombia. Growing up in South Florida, I've had my fair share of arepas, yet my aunt's are by far my favorite. The difference between Venezuelan and Colombian arepas is that Colombians usually mix cheese into the dough—I personally think it should be a requirement. For dinner I'll stuff them with braised beef or *carnitas* and top them with a salsa; for breakfast, I'll eat them plain with softened salted butter.

1. In a medium bowl, mix together the warm water, butter, and salt. Place the cornmeal in another bowl, making a well in the center. Pour the liquid into the well, mixing with your hands until thoroughly combined. At first the dough will stick to your hands; continue until it's soft and no longer sticky. Gently fold in the grated cheese. Cover with a damp towel and allow the dough to rest for 10 minutes.

2. Separate the dough into 8 balls. Place a ball onto the palm of your hand and, alternating the ball between your two hands, flatten the ball into a disk that is 3 inches in diameter and ¼ inch thick. If you wish, gently press around the disk to eliminate any cracks. Continue to make arepas with the remaining dough.

3. Place a skillet over medium-high heat, and brush with about a teaspoon of vegetable oil. Once the skillet is hot, add the arepas, being sure to not overcrowd the pan. Cook for 7 to 10 minutes on each side until golden brown. Transfer the cooked arepas to a preheated 200°F oven to keep warm. Repeat the process to cook the remaining arepas. Serve with a pat of butter on top, or slice the arepa in half horizontally, using a knife, and stuff with any kind of cheese or meat to your liking.

zucchini fritters

2 medium zucchini

Salt

3 tablespoons all-purpose flour

¼ teaspoon baking powder

¼ teaspoon cayenne pepper

1 large egg, lightly beaten

1 garlic clove, minced

Vegetable oil, for the skillet

GLUTEN-FREE

In late summer, I always end up with way more zucchini than I know what to do with. This abundance always has me on the search for new and different ways to use it up. These zucchini fritters have earned their place in my regular late-summer rotation; they're quick, light, and simple to put together. And as the seasons change from summer to fall, I love using this recipe as a template, swapping out the zucchini for other squashes like acorn and kabocha.

1. Using a hand grater, coarsely grate the zucchini, lengthwise. Transfer the zucchini to a bowl, sprinkle with ¼ teaspoon of salt and let stand for 5 minutes. Gather the zucchini in the center of a few layers of cheesecloth and squeeze out the excess water.

2. In a small bowl, whisk together the flour, baking powder, cayenne pepper, and ¼ teaspoon of salt. Place the dried zucchini into a medium bowl, along with the flour mixture, egg, and garlic. Mix until combined.

3. Place a skillet over medium-high heat, and pour in vegetable oil until it reaches ¼ inch up the sides. Once the oil is hot, for each fritter place a heaping tablespoon of the zucchini mixture into the skillet, slightly flattening it with the back of the spoon. Cook for 2 to 3 minutes until golden brown. Carefully flip and cook on the opposite side for 1 minute more. Transfer to paper towels to drain and then place them in a preheated 200°F oven to keep warm. Repeat the process to cook the remaining fritters. Serve immediately.

huaraches

1 cup powdered masa harina

½ teaspoon salt

¾ cup plus 2 tablespoons warm water

¼ cup refried beans (canned or homemade)

Vegetable oil, for the skillet

VEGAN AND
GLUTEN-FREE

Makes 4 huaraches

I first had *huaraches* at a Mexican restaurant in the Boyle Heights part of Los Angeles called Antojitos Carmen. The dough, similar to tortillas, is shaped into a ball and then stuffed with a small amount of refried beans. After being rolled out and cooked, it takes a short trip to the skillet for a light fry to achieve a golden, crispy crust. I've had them topped with meats like *al pastor, barbacoa,* and *carnitas*—and I think they're delicious, but when zucchini is in abundance, I love topping them with delicate zucchini blossoms, crumbled queso fresco, and a good spicy salsa.

1. In a medium bowl, mix together the masa, salt, and warm water. Cover the bowl with plastic wrap and allow the dough to rest for 10 minutes.

2. Add the refried beans to the bowl of a food processor and pulse until the beans become a paste. Alternatively, you could mash them with a fork.

3. Separate the dough into 4 balls. Roll each ball into an oval shape. Using your thumb, make a long, deep well in the center. It will resemble the shape of a cigar. Place 1 scant teaspoon of the beans into the well. Pinch the cavity closed, enclosing the beans completely.

4. One at a time place each piece of filled dough between two pieces of plastic wrap. Using a rolling pin, lightly press into a 4-inch-long oval that is ¼ inch thick.

5. Preheat your skillet over medium-high heat and brush with ½ teaspoon of vegetable oil. Add the huaraches and cook for 1 to 2

minutes on each side, flipping when lightly golden brown. Continue until all 4 huaraches are cooked. Remove from skillet and set aside.

6. Place the skillet over medium-high heat, and pour in vegetable oil until it reaches ½ inch up the sides. Once the oil is hot, carefully add the huaraches to the pan and fry for 1 to 2 minutes, until golden brown on each side. Gently turn and cook on the opposite sides for 1 to 2 minutes more. Transfer to paper towels to drain. Serve hot.

duck fat corn cakes

Makes 8 corn cakes

One of my all-time favorite side dishes is smashed herb potatoes fried in duck fat. Using it in pancakes might seem a little insane and overly decadent, but duck fat actually has a nutritional value similar to olive oil. The duck fat gives these pancakes rich, full flavor, while the corn adds a gritty texture. To mellow out the richness, I recommend pairing them with something tart; think sour cherries or cranberry chutney.

1. In a medium bowl, mix together the flour, cornmeal, baking powder, and salt.
2. In a measuring cup or small bowl, measure out the milk. Add the egg and duck fat and beat until combined.
3. All at once, add the wet ingredients to the dry ingredients and mix until just combined. The batter should have some small to medium lumps.
4. Preheat your skillet, over medium heat and melt 1 teaspoon of duck fat. Using a ¼-cup measure, scoop the batter onto the warm skillet. Cook for 2 to 3 minutes until small bubbles form on the surface of the pancakes and then flip. Reduce the heat to medium-low and cook on the opposite sides for 1 to 2 minutes, or until golden brown.
5. Transfer the cooked pancakes to a baking sheet and place in a preheated 200°F oven to keep warm. Repeat the process with the remaining batter.
6. To make the cranberry chutney: Add the cranberries, sugar, orange juice, ginger, and a pinch of salt to a small saucepan. Cook over medium heat for 10 to 12 minutes, until the cranberries pop. Fold in the dried cherries. Serve warm over the corn cakes.

DRY MIX

¾ cup all-purpose flour

½ cup cornmeal

1 tablespoon baking powder

⅛ teaspoon salt

WET MIX

¾ cup whole milk

1 large egg

1 tablespoon duck fat, melted

CRANBERRY CHUTNEY

I cup fresh or frozen cranberries

¼ cup sugar

1 tablespoon orange juice, freshly squeezed

¼ teaspoon fresh ginger, peeled and finely grated

Pinch of salt

2 tablespoons dried cherries

Duck fat, for the skillet

scattered, smothered, and covered hash brown cakes

1 pound russet potatoes, peeled

Kosher salt

¼ cup vegetable oil

2 shallots, minced

½ cup sharp cheddar cheese, grated

Freshly ground black pepper

Vegetable oil, for the skillet

GLUTEN-FREE

Makes 12 hash brown cakes

Going to college in Winston-Salem, North Carolina, meant late-night meals took place at Waffle House. My go-to was the famous "scattered, smothered, and covered." If you're unfamiliar, allow me to enlighten you of its glory. It begins with the "scatter," which is the potatoes hitting the hot oil and pan; then the "smother," another word for the onions being thrown atop the potatoes; lastly, the "covered," a slice of American cheese delicately placed on the crispy potatoes. My version is slightly different. I changed the shape to resemble more of a latke. I also use shallots—I favor the subtle flavor in this case. And I swapped out the American cheese for a good-quality sharp cheddar cheese. But honestly, if you wanted to use good ol' American cheese, I'd totally understand.

1. Using a hand grater, coarsely grate the potatoes, lengthwise. Transfer the potatoes to a bowl, sprinkle with ¼ teaspoon of salt, and let stand for 5 minutes. Gather the potatoes in the center of a few layers of cheesecloth and squeeze out the excess water.

2. In a skillet over medium-high heat, heat the vegetable oil. When the oil is hot, for each cake add a heaping tablespoon of the dried grated potatoes to the skillet, flattening it slightly; season each cake with a dash of salt. Add a pinch of minced shallot atop the cake and cook for 1 minute, or until the edge of the potato turns golden brown. Add a small handful of grated cheese to each cake and cover with a lid for 1 to 2 minutes more, until the cheese has melted.

3. Transfer to paper towels to drain and then place them in a preheated 200°F oven to keep warm. Repeat the process with the remaining potatoes, shallots, and grated cheese. Serve immediately.

cheddar chive popovers

Vegetable oil or cooking spray for the muffin pan

BATTER

1½ cups all-purpose flour

¾ teaspoon salt

3 large eggs, at room temperature

1½ cups whole milk, at room temperature

1 tablespoon fresh chives, minced

1 cup sharp cheddar, finely grated

Popovers are the drama queens of the carb world. When these cheesy pillows appear from the oven, they're tall, a beautiful yellow hue, and speckled with green chives. With their hollow, cheesy-custard centers, these popovers are pretty perfect on their own. I can assure you that four of them, and a glass of wine, has been dinner on multiple occasions. The only thing I can think of that would make them better is a dip in hot soup on a chilly night.

1. Preheat the oven to 350°F. Generously coat a muffin pan with the vegetable oil or spray and set aside.

2. In a medium bowl, combine the flour and salt. In a measuring cup, measure out milk, add the eggs, and beat until combined.

3. Pour the wet ingredients into the dry ingredients and mix until nearly smooth. The batter will be thin with a few lumps. Fold in ½ cup of the cheddar cheese and the chives. If you'd like, you can transfer the batter to a large measuring cup or bowl with a spout; this will make it easier to pour the batter into the muffin wells.

5. Preheat the muffin pan in the oven for 2 to 3 minutes. Remove the hot pan and carefully pour the batter into each well, filling them a little more than halfway. Top with the remaining ½ cup of cheddar cheese. Bake for 30 to 35 minutes until tall, puffed, and golden brown.

cheddar bacon pancakes

I'm a huge advocate of "brinner" a.k.a. breakfast for dinner. If you are, too, then these Cheddar Bacon Pancakes are just the thing for you. The salty bacon and sharp cheddar are pretty awesome with a heavy pour of dreamy maple syrup.

1. In a medium bowl, mix together the flour, cornmeal, baking powder, baking soda, and salt.

2. Measure out the buttermilk in a measuring cup or small bowl. Add the egg and beat until thoroughly combined.

3. All at once, add the wet ingredients to the dry ingredients and mix until just combined. The batter should have some small to medium lumps. Gently fold in the diced bacon and cheddar cheese.

4. Preheat your skillet over medium heat and brush with 1½ teaspoons of butter or a teaspoon of vegetable oil. Using a ¼-cup measure, scoop the batter onto the warm skillet. Cook for 2 to 3 minutes until small bubbles form on the surface of the pancakes, and then flip. Reduce the heat to medium-low and cook on the opposite sides for 1 to 2 minutes, or until golden brown.

5. Transfer the cooked pancakes to a baking sheet and place in a preheated 200°F oven to keep warm. Repeat the process with the remaining batter. Serve immediately.

DRY MIX

1 cup all-purpose flour

1 tablespoon cornmeal

1 teaspoon baking powder

1 teaspoon baking soda

⅛ teaspoon salt

WET MIX

1 cup plus 2 tablespoons buttermilk, shaken

1 large egg

MIX-INS

3 slices bacon, cooked and diced

¼ cup cheddar cheese, grated

Butter or vegetable oil, for the skillet

socca with harissa aioli

SOCCA

½ cup chickpea flour

¼ teaspoon salt

¼ teaspoon ground cumin

¾ cup water, warm

3 tablespoons olive oil

HARISSA AIOLI

½ cup mayonnaise

1 teaspoon harissa

Makes 1 socca

Socca can typically be found on the streets of Nice, France. Think of it almost like a crispy crêpe made from chickpea flour. Their easy assembly and baking, make them ideal to serve as a snack or appetizer. I like to cut the socca into small diamonds and serve it with whatever dipping sauce I can whip together using what's in my fridge. In this case, I paired it with a spicy harissa aioli.

1. In a large bowl, mix together the chickpea flour, salt, and cumin. Pour in the water and 2 tablespoons of the olive oil; mix just until combined. The batter will be really thin. Cover the batter with plastic wrap and allow it to rest for 15 minutes.

2. Preheat the oven to 450°F for 2 to 3 minutes. Place a 10-inch cast-iron skillet in the oven to preheat.

3. Carefully remove the hot skillet from the oven. Add a teaspoon of olive oil to the pan and swirl it around until hot. Pour the batter into the hot pan and bake for 8 to 10 minutes until the socca turns a light golden brown and edges are crispy.

4. Gently flip the socca and cook on the opposite side for 2 minutes. Cut into wedges or squares and serve.

5. To make the aioli: Mix together the mayonnaise and harissa until well combined.

bacon-wrapped meat loaf cakes

Makes 7 cakes

1 tablespoon olive oil

¼ yellow onion, diced (about ½ cup)

2 garlic cloves, minced

1 pound ground beef chuck

1 tablespoon Worcestershire sauce

1 tablespoon tomato paste

1½ tablespoons fresh flat-leaf parsley, minced

1 teaspoon kosher salt

½ teaspoon crushed red pepper flakes

¼ cup plain dry bread crumbs

1 large egg

7 slices thin bacon, cut in half crosswise

2½ tablespoons ketchup

I didn't have meat loaf until a few years ago. People always freak out when I tell them this, but growing up my mom only had a few American dishes in rotation, and meat loaf was definitely not one of them. At first bite, I didn't think I had missed much. I later found out—after I had experienced a good version—that meat loaf should be full of flavor, moist throughout, and fluffy. Meat loaf wrapped in bacon doesn't hurt either. I like making it in individual patties; I kind of think it helps with what I like to call "cute-ifying" an otherwise mound of baked ground beef.

1. Preheat the oven to 325°F. In a medium skillet, heat the olive oil over medium heat. Add the onions and cook until translucent, 5 to 7 minutes. Place the minced garlic atop the onions and cook until fragrant, about 1 minute more.
2. In a medium bowl, add the cooked onion mixture, ground beef, Worcestershire sauce, tomato paste, parsley, salt, pepper flakes, bread crumbs, and egg. Using your hands, combine mixture with a gentle touch, until everything is incorporated.
3. Scoop 2 heaping tablespoons of the ground beef mixture onto the palm of your hand and shape the meat into a patty. It should weigh a little over 3 ounces. Continue making patties with the remaining mixture.
4. Wrap each patty with two halves of the bacon strips, placing them side by side and tucking them under the patty. Transfer the patties to a lined baking sheet and bake for 20 minutes. Remove baking sheet from the oven and top each patty with a heaping teaspoon of ketchup. Return to the oven for 10 minutes more, or until the internal temperature registers 160°F.

beet crêpes

Makes 8 crêpes

BEETS

1 medium beet

2 tablespoons water

BATTER

2 large eggs

1 cup whole milk

¼ cup beet liquid

2 tablespoons unsalted butter, melted and cooled

1 cup all-purpose flour

¼ teaspoon salt

Vegetable oil, for the crêpe pan

I'm not what you call a beet lover. Sure, they're alright in a salad, but only when smothered in goat cheese. I do, however, love them in baked goods. I first fell in love with them, used in this way, when I tried a beet vegan cupcake. And I had my first beet (and quinoa) pancake experience when I made a recipe from Kim Boyce's beautiful cookbook, *Good to the Grain*. Her recipe calls for roasting the beets, caramelizing their sugars, which in turn adds incredible flavor to the pancake. I took that method and applied it to a crêpe. The bright, pink hue is breathtaking, while the subtle sweetness, along with earthy flavor is delicious. Feel free to fill this crêpe with any combination of things, such as sautéed seasonal vegetables like zucchini, eggplant, or asparagus. My all-time favorite is a small ball of soft burrata, crispy lardons, topped with fresh, peppery arugula.

1. Preheat the oven to 400°F. Place the beet with the water in an oven-proof ceramic dish and cover the dish with aluminum foil. Roast the beet until tender, about 45 minutes. Peel and trim the roasted beet and cut it into cubes. Add to a food processor with ½ cup of water and process until combined. Run the liquified beets through a sieve. Discard the solids and reserve ¼ cup of the beet liquid.

2. To the jar of a blender, add the eggs, milk, reserved beet liquid, and melted butter and pulse for a few seconds until liquids are combined. Add the flour and salt. Pulse for 10 seconds or so and until the flour is incorporated, being sure not to overblend. Transfer the batter to a bowl and cover with plastic wrap. Place the batter in the refrigerator for an hour to rest.

3. Place a crêpe pan over medium heat. Brush the skillet with a light coating of oil. Add 2 ounces of batter to the center of the pan and swirl it around until the bottom is coated evenly. Cook until the

edges of the crêpe pull away from the pan, 1 to 2 minutes. Carefully flip and cook on the opposite side for another 30 seconds; you may have to play with the temperature a bit. The common notion is that the first crêpe goes to the pan, so don't get discouraged if you have to try a few times to get the temperature right. Transfer the cooked crêpes to a baking sheet and place in a preheated 200°F oven to keep warm. Repeat the process with the remaining batter.

buckwheat crêpes

2 large eggs

1 cup whole milk

¼ cup water

1 tablespoon unsalted
butter, melted and
cooled

½ cup all-purpose
flour

½ cup buckwheat
flour

¼ teaspoon salt

Vegetable oil, for the
crêpe pan

Makes 8 crêpes

I would like you to close your eyes. I'll wait. You're on the cobblestone streets of Brittany, France, wearing your cutest "I'm in France so I'm going to look French" outfit and you just entered a crêperie, you know, the one you Googled, found on a random blog that swears it's a locals-only place. And since, "when in Rome . . ." you order the quintessential "I'm in France crêpe" and go with the galette. Smart move. They serve it piping hot, smothered in melted Gruyère cheese, a fried egg, and a heavy-hand of salty ham. You take your first bite . . . it's heaven. But you're confused by the earthy flavor from the crêpe. You inquire and you find out it's buckwheat. Buckwheat?! There's no heaviness?! Just a thin, light-as-a-feather crêpe with a good punch of nuttiness. What a dream. If you're into re-creating that scene right here and now (cute outfit included), I suggest you make these. Like, now.

1. To the jar of a blender, add the eggs, milk, water, and melted butter and pulse for a few seconds until the liquids are combined. Add the all-purpose flour, buckwheat flour, and salt. Pulse for 10 seconds or so and until the flour is incorporated, being careful not to overblend. Transfer the batter to a bowl and cover with plastic wrap. Place the batter in the refrigerator for an hour to rest.

2. Place a crêpe pan over medium heat. Brush the pan with a light coating of oil. Add 2 ounces of batter to the center of the pan and swirl it around until the bottom is coated evenly. Cook until the edges of the crêpe pull away from the pan, 1 to 2 minutes. Carefully flip and cook on the opposite side for another 30 seconds; you may have to play with the temperature a bit. The common notion is that the first crêpe goes to the pan, so don't get discouraged if you have to try a few times to get the temperature right. Transfer the cooked crêpes to a baking sheet and place in a preheated 200°F oven to keep warm. Repeat the process with the remaining batter.

gruyère and ham dutch baby

3 large eggs, room temperature

⅔ cup whole milk, at room temperature

⅔ cup all-purpose flour

⅛ teaspoon salt

¾ cup Gruyère cheese, grated

½ cup cubed ham, cut into ½-inch pieces

4 tablespoons (½ stick) unsalted butter, cubed

HEADS-UP

When you take this beauty out of the oven, it will be beautifully puffy and golden brown, but will quickly deflate. Don't fret! Simply slice it up and enjoy.

Makes one 10-inch Dutch baby

This Dutch baby reminds me of my favorite bistro French sandwich, the Croque Monsieur. Sure, there isn't any béchamel sauce, but you don't miss it one bit. The crispy edges, the Gruyère cheesy center, and bits of salty ham are pretty perfect, especially when paired with a side salad and a few glasses of crisp wine.

1. Preheat the oven to 400°F. Place a 10-inch cast-iron skillet in the oven to preheat for 2 to 3 minutes.

2. Meanwhile, in a bowl, whisk together the eggs and milk, until thoroughly combined and the mixture turns a pale yellow. Add the flour and salt and whisk until lumps are barely visible, and the batter is thin. Fold in ½ cup of the Gruyère and ¼ cup of the ham.

3. Carefully take the hot skillet out of the oven, place the butter inside, and swirl it around until it's melted. Pour the batter into the skillet and return to the oven. At the 8-minute mark, when the Dutch baby begins to puff up and turn a light golden brown color, open the oven and carefully add the remaining grated cheese and ham to the center, sprinkling it evenly. Bake for 7 to 8 minutes more until the edges are golden brown and the Dutch baby is puffed and tall. Serve immediately.

crab cakes with citrus tartar sauce

Makes 8 crab cakes

CRAB CAKES

Olive oil

½ shallot, minced

1 pound lump crabmeat

2 large eggs

1 teaspoon Worcestershire sauce

1 teaspoon Old Bay Seasoning

½ teaspoon finely grated lemon zest

1 teaspoon freshly squeezed lemon juice

¼ teaspoon hot sauce (I use Tapatío)

2 tablespoons fresh flat-leaf parsley, minced

2 tablespoons mayonnaise

1¼ cups Ritz crackers, crushed

Vegetable oil, for the skillet

My dad's best friend Charles comes from a long lineage of South Carolina crab fishermen. This recipe has been in his family for generations and he was nice enough to pass it along to me. I adapted it slightly, tweaking and adding only a few things here and there. My favorite part, hands down, is the use of Ritz crackers in place of bread crumbs. The buttery crackers work wonders with the rich crabmeat.

1. In a small skillet, over medium heat, heat a teaspoon of olive oil. When the oil is hot, add the minced shallot and cook until translucent, about 3 minutes. Set aside.

2. Place the crabmeat in between a few layers of cheesecloth and wring out any excess liquid. Transfer the crabmeat to a bowl. Add the eggs, Worcestershire sauce, salt, Old Bay Seasoning, lemon zest, lemon juice, hot sauce, parsley, mayonnaise, and crushed Ritz crackers. Mix until thoroughly combined. Cover the bowl with plastic wrap and transfer to the refrigerator to chill for 1 hour.

3. Scoop 2 tablespoons of the crab mixture onto the palm of your hand. Form into a patty about 3 inches in diameter, and ¾ inch thick. Repeat the process with the remaining mixture.

4. Place a skillet over medium-high heat, and pour in vegetable oil until it reaches ½ inch up the sides. Once the oil is hot, carefully add the crab cakes, being careful not to overcrowd the skillet. Cook for 2 to 3 minutes until golden brown. Gently flip and cook on the opposite sides for a minute or two. Transfer to paper towels to drain

CITRUS TARTAR
SAUCE

½ cup mayonnaise

3 cornichons, diced

1 tablespoon capers,
chopped

½ teaspoon finely
grated lemon zest

1 tablespoon freshly
squeezed lemon juice

Salt

and then place them in a preheated 200°F oven to keep warm.
Repeat the process to cook the remaining cakes. Serve immediately
with tartar sauce.

5. To make the Citrus Tartar Sauce: In a small bowl, mix all of the
    ingredients together until combined. Season with salt to taste.

kimchi fritters }

Makes 8 fritters

This might seem silly, but I get really nervous when I cook for my friends. This has a lot to do with the fact that most of them are incredible cooks and chefs themselves. I was especially terrified of feeding these kimchi pancakes to my friend, food stylist, and Korean food pro, Jenny Park. When she took her first bite and nodded, I was pretty pumped. I made a few tweaks based on her comments and suggestions, and the pro-tip on where and how to buy kimchi is all hers.

1. In a medium bowl, mix together the kimchi, flour, water, kimchi juice, scallions, and salt.
2. Place a skillet over medium-high heat, and pour in vegetable oil until it reaches ¼ inch up the sides. Once the oil is hot, for each fritter scoop 2 tablespoons of the kimchi mixture into the skillet, flattening each slightly with the back of the spoon. Cook for 2 to 3 minutes, until crispy and golden brown. Gently flip and cook on the opposite sides for a minute or two. Transfer to paper towels to drain and then place them in a preheated 200°F oven to keep warm. Repeat the process to make the remaining fritters. Serve immediately.
3. To make the dipping sauce: Add the soy sauce, sesame oil, and scallions to a small bowl and mix to combine. Top with a sprinkling of sesame seeds.

FRITTERS

1 cup store-bought kimchi, drained and chopped

½ cup all-purpose flour

¼ cup water

¼ cup kimchi juice

¼ cup minced scallions

½ teaspoon kosher salt

Vegetable oil, for the skillet

DIPPING SAUCE

½ cup soy sauce

1 teaspoon sesame oil

1 tablespoon minced scallions

½ teaspoon sesame seeds

VEGAN

PRO-TIP

You can find kimchi at most grocery stores; however, the best kimchi is typically found in Korean markets. Search out kimchi that comes in a plastic bag (versus a jar) that's marked "Made in Korea." This is shipped directly from Korea quickly—and usually has the best flavor. Try to buy kimchi that is labeled "Mat Kimchi," which comes presliced, making it ideal for these fritters.

133

spinach pancakes

SPINACH JUICE

4 cups fresh spinach,
washed and drained

DRY MIX

1 cup all-purpose flour

1 tablespoon baking
powder

½ teaspoon finely
grated lemon zest

½ teaspoon kosher
salt

WET MIX

½ cup whole milk

¼ cup plus 2
tablespoons spinach
juice

1 large egg

Vegetable oil, for the
skillet

Makes 8 pancakes

Butter and sugar are staples in my life. This is a fact. But I'm a Libra, and though I don't really believe in horoscopes, people tell me my need for balance can be attributed to this. I suppose this can explain my obsession for juicing fruits and vegetables. I'd take drinking vegetables over eating them any day! These pancakes get their beautiful green hue thanks to spinach juice, and the lemon zest contributes a bright, fresh flavor.

1. To a juice extractor, add the spinach and ¼ cup water. Process until juice is produced. Set aside ¼ cup plus 2 tablespoons of the spinach juice.
2. In a medium bowl, mix together the all-purpose flour, baking powder, lemon zest, and salt.
3. In a measuring cup or small bowl, measure out the milk. Add the spinach juice and egg and beat until thoroughly combined.
4. All at once, add the wet ingredients to the dry ingredients and mix until just combined. The batter should have some small to medium lumps.
5. Preheat your skillet over medium heat and brush with 1 teaspoon of oil. Using a ¼-cup measure, scoop the batter onto the warm skillet. Cook for 2 to 3 minutes until small bubbles form on the surface of the pancakes, and then flip. Reduce heat to medium-low and cook on the opposite sides for 1 to 2 minutes, or until golden brown.
6. Transfer the cooked pancakes to a baking sheet and place them in a preheated 200°F oven to keep warm. Repeat the process with the remaining batter. Serve immediately.

garlic and parmesan popovers

Wherever there's a garlic knot, pasta is close by. Perhaps this is why my love for garlic knots runs so deep. Whatever the case may be, I really can't get enough of them. These popovers—sans kneading and rises—are the perfect quick-fix. When these popovers exit the oven, they get doused with bits of garlic, fresh parsley, olive oil, and Parmesan cheese. Just like a garlic knot, but without the fuss.

1. Preheat the oven to 350°F. Generously coat a muffin pan with vegetable oil or spray and set aside.
2. In a medium bowl, combine the flour and salt. In a measuring cup, measure out the milk, add the eggs, and beat until combined.
3. All at once, pour the wet ingredients into the dry ingredients and mix until nearly smooth. The batter will be thin with a few lumps. Fold in 1 tablespoon of minced garlic and ¼ cup of the grated cheese. If you'd like, you can transfer the batter to a large measuring cup or bowl with a spout; this will make it easier to pour the batter into the muffin wells.
4. Preheat the muffin pan in the oven for 2 to 3 minutes. Remove the hot pan and carefully pour the batter into each well, filling them a little more than halfway. Bake for 30 to 35 minutes until tall, puffed, and golden brown.
5. While the popovers are baking, mix together the topping. In a small bowl, combine the remaining minced garlic, the remaining ¼ cup grated cheese, the parsley, and olive oil. When the popovers come out of the oven, top each one with a scant teaspoon of the topping mixture. Serve immediately.

Vegetable oil or cooking spray for the muffin pan

BATTER

1½ cups all-purpose flour

1 teaspoon kosher salt

1½ cups whole milk, at room temperature

3 large eggs, at room temperature

5 garlic cloves, minced

½ cup Parmigiano-Reggiano, finely grated

4 tablespoons fresh flat-leaf parsley, minced

2 tablespoons olive oil, plus 1 teaspoon

curried cauliflower fritters

1 head cauliflower, cut into florets

2 tablespoons olive oil

Salt

½ cup dry bread crumbs

2 large eggs

2 tablespoons all-purpose flour

2 tablespoons Greek plain yogurt

1½ teaspoons madras curry powder

1 teaspoon ground cumin

½ teaspoon ground turmeric

¼ teaspoon ground cinnamon

Vegetable oil, for the skillet

Makes about 10 fritters (Note: Heads of cauliflower size may vary so it might make 11. Mine weighed about 1 pound.)

When I was little I'd call cauliflower "little trees." I loved eating the "little trees" as a kid, and as I've gotten older they continue to be one of my favorite vegetables to cook with. I've learned that cauliflower, with its mild, slightly sweet, and nutty flavor, is the perfect canvas to show off some of my favorite stronger flavors. In this case it does a lovely job with curry. These fritters come together with ease; the crunch from the cauliflower makes them fun to eat, while the curry gives them rich, deep flavor. During the months of February and March, I love making these fritters with purple and bright green cauliflower. Who knew cauliflower could be so beautiful.

1. Preheat oven to 400°F. Place the cauliflower on a lined baking sheet and drizzle with the olive oil. Season the cauliflower with 1 teaspoon of salt and transfer to the oven for 20 minutes, turning once to ensure even roasting.

2. Transfer the cauliflower to a food processor and pulse until the mixture is coarsely ground.

3. Place the cauliflower in a large bowl and add bread crumbs, eggs, flour, yogurt, curry powder, cumin, turmeric, cinnamon, and ¼ teaspoon salt. Mix until thoroughly combined. Cover the bowl with plastic wrap and transfer to the refrigerator to chill for 3 hours.

4. Scoop 2 tablespoons of the cauliflower mixture into the palm of your hand. Form into a patty 3 inches in diameter and ¾ inch thick. Continue to make parties with the remaining mixture.

5. Place a skillet over medium-high heat, and pour in vegetable oil until it reaches ½ inch up the sides. Once the oil is hot, carefully add the fritters, being sure to not overcrowd the pan. Cook for 2 to 3 minutes until golden brown. Gently flip and cook on the opposite sides for a minute or two. Transfer to paper towels to drain and then place them in a preheated 200°F oven to keep warm. Repeat the process to cook the remaining fritters. Serve immediately.

llapingachos

3 medium (1.5 lbs) russet potatoes, peeled and cubed

1 teaspoon olive oil

2 shallots, minced

2 garlic cloves, minced

1 teaspoon ground cumin

1 teaspoon ground paprika

Kosher salt

Freshly ground black pepper

1 large egg yolk, beaten

½ cup low-moisture mozzarella cheese, grated

Vegetable oil, for the skillet

When I came across a recipe for Ecuadorian *Llapingachos,* I felt like I had found gold. As I read further, I realized they're basically just mashed potato pancakes, which I think is pretty genius. Mashed potatoes might be one of my favorite dishes to cozy up to. If you're on the mashed potato bandwagon, then I'm pretty certain these things have your name written all over them. They have a slightly crispy exterior and soft, pillow interior, filled with melted cheese.

1. Place the potatoes in a large pot of boiling salted water and cook until tender, about 10 minutes. Drain and set aside.

2. In a small skillet, heat a teaspoon of olive oil over medium heat, add the shallots and cook until translucent, about 3 minutes. Add the garlic atop the shallots and cook until fragrant, about 1 minute.

3. Press the potatoes through a ricer or, alternatively, mash them by using a stand mixer fitted with the paddle attachment. Mix in the cooked shallots, cumin, and paprika. Season with salt and pepper to taste. (I used about ½ teaspoon of salt and ¼ teaspoon of pepper.) Fold in the egg yolk, cover the bowl with plastic wrap, and refrigerate for 2 hours.

4. For each llapingacho, scoop 2 tablespoons of the potato mixture into the palm of your hand. Make a large well in the center, using your finger, and place a teaspoon of cheese into the middle. Pinch the cavity closed and gently press the ball, forming a ½-inch-thick disk. Continue making llapingachos with the remaining mixture.

5. Preheat the oven to 200°F. Place a skillet over medium-high heat and lightly brush the pan with vegetable oil. Once the skillet is hot, add the llapinagachos. Cook for 2 to 3 minutes until golden brown. Gently flip and cook on the opposite sides for a minute or two. Transfer to the oven to keep warm. Repeat the process to cook the remaining llapingachos. Serve immediately.

TOPPINGS

I used to be the person who strictly wanted a pat of
butter and a small drizzle of warm maple syrup atop my
pancakes. But over the years, I stepped out of my boring
(yet delicious) routine and tried new toppings, like
lemon- and sugar-soaked fruits, and liquor- and fruit-
spiked syrups, and never looked back.

berry butters ⎬

It doesn't get much easier than this! A gentle mix of softened butter with fresh berries gives you flavorful, fresh-tasting butter that's not only pretty to look at but also delicious to eat.

1. To the bowl of a food processor, add the butter, fresh berries, and salt. Pulse for 30 seconds, until the berries are smashed and combined with the butter. The berry butter may be served right away.

PRO-TIP

If you'd like to make this in advance, transfer the butter mixture to the center of a sheet of plastic wrap and roll it into a log, twisting the ends to seal the log. Transfer to the refrigerator until you're ready to serve.

8 tablespoons (1 stick) unsalted butter, at room temperature

¼ cup fresh berries, cleaned and trimmed

Pinch of kosher salt

HEADS-UP

Fresh berries like raspberries, blueberries, or blackberries work best. If you want to use frozen berries, be sure to defrost and drain them in order to rid them of any excess water.

mascerated fruit

1 cup berries or fruit,
cleaned and trimmed

2 tablespoons freshly
squeezed lemon juice

2 tablespoons sugar

VEGAN AND
GLUTEN-FREE

Makes ¾ cup

Use any berries you like for this! Or even better, use a mix.

1. In a small bowl, stir together the berries, lemon juice, and sugar. Allow to stand at room temperature for 30 minutes, and until juices are released.

2. For firmer berries like blueberries and blackberries, at the 30-minute mark, mash the berries with the back of the fork and allow to sit for an additional 15 minutes.

PRO-TIP

You can up the ante with this mascerated fruit by adding a tablespoon or two of liqueurs like Grand Marnier or St. Germain. Extracts like vanilla or almond are also a nice addition.

blueberry maple syrup

1 cup fresh or frozen
blueberries

¼ cup sugar

⅓ cup water

¼ cup pure maple
syrup

VEGAN AND
GLUTEN-FREE

Makes 1 cup syrup

This blueberry syrup is my favorite thing to pour on top of plain, buttermilk pancakes. It's tart, sweet, and comes together in a snap.

1. To a small saucepan over medium-low heat, add blueberries, sugar and water. Cook until soft, 5 to 7 minutes, stirring occasionally and mashing the blueberries with the back of a spoon.

2. Add maple syrup and cook for 3 minutes more. Though the blueberries will cook down, they'll still have some shape. If you'd like smooth syrup, you can transfer the mixture to a food processor and pulse until smooth. I personally love it with bits of blueberry.

cream cheese glaze

8 ounces cream
cheese, at room
temperature

½ cup confectioners'
sugar

⅔ cup whole milk

⅛ teaspoon pure
vanilla extract

GLUTEN-FREE

Makes 1 cup glaze

This cream cheese glaze is awesome poured atop the Carrot Cake Pancakes (page 34) and Red Velvet Silver Dollars (page 26).

1. In a medium bowl, add cream cheese, sugar, milk, and vanilla. Using an electric mixer, beat until smooth. Serve immediately.

blood orange syrup

Makes ¾ cup syrup

1 cup freshly squeezed
blood orange juice

2 tablespoons sugar

3 teaspoons corn-
starch

Pinch of salt

When January rolls around, winter citrus is abundant and I go crazy! In this case I used blood oranges, but feel free to swap it out for other citrus like Meyer lemons, grapefruit, or navel oranges.

VEGAN AND
GLUTEN-FREE

1. To a small saucepan over medium-high heat, add the blood orange juice and sugar. Once the sugar has dissolved, whisk in the corn-starch. Cook for 8 to 10 minutes until thickened. Add the salt and serve immediately.

bourbon maple syrup

Makes ¾ cup syrup

1 cup pure maple syrup

2 tablespoons unsalted butter

2 tablespoons bourbon

Pinch of salt

GLUTEN-FREE

There's bourbon and butter in this maple syrup. Enough said.

1. To a small saucepan over moderately high heat, add the maple syrup and butter. Bring the mixture to a boil and immediately lower the heat to low, and cook for 5 minutes, stirring often, until slightly reduced. Using a spoon, skim the foam from the surface and discard. Stir in the bourbon and the salt and cook for an additional minute. Serve warm.

avocado butter

Makes ¾ cup butter

I first made this Avocado Butter for putting on top of hard-shell tacos. I think it's a great addition to the Spicy Black Bean Cakes (page 88), Jalapeño Corn Cakes (page 82) and Empera's Arepas (page 106).

1. To the bowl of a food processor, add the avocado, sour cream, lime juice, lime zest, and cumin. Pulse until smooth. Add salt and pepper to taste. Serve immediately.

4 ripe Haas avocadoes

½ cup sour cream

¼ cup freshly squeezed lime juice

½ teaspoon finely grated lime zest

¼ teaspoon ground cumin

Salt and freshly ground black pepper

GLUTEN-FREE

roasted shallot aioli

2 shallots
1 tablespoon olive oil
Salt
Freshly ground black pepper
1 cup mayonnaise
½ teaspoon finely grated lemon zest

GLUTEN-FREE

When roasted, shallots get all caramelized and take on a delicious, slightly sweet flavor. Here they are blended with mayonnaise, some lemon zest, and salt and pepper. Pair this with the Curried Cauliflower Fritters (page 138).

1. Preheat the oven to 400°F. Slice off the tops of each shallot, discarding the scraps. Transfer the shallots to the center of a piece of aluminum foil. Pour the olive oil on top of each shallot and sprinkle liberally with salt and pepper. Wrap the shallots in the foil and transfer to a baking sheet. Roast in the oven for 30 to 40 minutes. Let cool.

2. Take the shallots out of their papery husks and add them to a food processor, along with the mayonnaise and lemon zest. Pulse until smooth. Add salt and pepper to taste. Serve immediately, or store in the refrigerator, in an airtight container for up to 2 weeks.

index